LIFE
IN THE
KINGDOM

*Foundations
of the
Faith*

Jack W. Hayford
with
John Amstutz

THOMAS NELSON PUBLISHERS
Nashville

CONTENTS

Life in the Kingdom: Foundations of the Faith is one of a series of study guides that focus exciting, discovery-geared coverage of Bible book and power themes—all prompting toward dynamic, Holy Spirit-filled living.

About the General Editor

JACK W. HAYFORD, noted pastor, teacher, writer, and composer, is the General Editor of the complete series, working with the publisher in the conceiving and developing of each of the books.

Dr. Hayford is Senior Pastor of The Church On The Way, the First Foursquare Church of Van Nuys, California. He and his wife, Anna, have four married children, all of whom are active in either pastoral ministry or vital church life. As General Editor of the *Spirit-Filled Life Bible*, Pastor Hayford led a four-year project, which has resulted in the availability of one of today's most practical and popular study Bibles. He is author of more than twenty books, including *A Passion for Fullness*, *The Beauty of Spiritual Language*, *Rebuilding the Real You*, and *Prayer Is Invading the Impossible*. His musical compositions number over four hundred songs, including the widely sung "Majesty."

About the Writer

JOHN AMSTUTZ has been in public ministry for over thirty years and still impresses his audience as a young, vibrant minister. His work as a pastor (Missionary Church), as a missionary (Jamaica Theological Seminary), as a church consultant (Southern California College, Charles E. Fuller Institute), and professor of Bible and Missions (LIFE Bible College) evidence the versatility of this gifted man. He is a graduate in physics from Point Loma College and received his M.Div. and D.Min. from Fuller Theological Seminary.

John is married to Doreen (nee Krueger) and they have four children: two married daughters, Colleen Powers and Renee Titus; and daughter Julie and son John, who are respectively graduated from and studying at LIFE Bible College.

Of this contributor the General Editor has remarked: "John's academic, ministerial, and spiritual pedigree—with the evidence of his strong family—says it all. This man is an elder to elders in the church, with a heartwarming way of presenting the truth for practical application."

THE KEYS
THAT KEEP ON FREEING

Is there anything that holds more mystery or more genuine practicality than a key? The mystery: "What does it fit? What can it turn on? What might it open? What new discovery could be made? The practicality: Something *will* most certainly open to the possessor! Something *will* absolutely be found to unlock and allow a possibility otherwise obstructed!

- Keys describe the instruments we use to access or ignite.
- Keys describe the concepts that unleash mind-boggling possibilities.
- Keys describe the different structures of musical notes which allow variation and range.

Jesus spoke of keys: "And I will give you the keys of the kingdom of heaven, and whatever you bind on earth will be bound in heaven, and whatever you loose on earth will be loosed in heaven" (Matt. 16:19).

While there is no conclusive list of exactly what keys Jesus was referring to, it is clear that He did confer upon His church—upon *all* who believe—the access to a realm of spiritual partnership with Him in the dominion of His kingdom. Faithful students of the Word of God, moving in the practical grace and biblical wisdom of Holy Spirit-filled living and ministry, have noted some of the primary themes which undergird this order of "spiritual partnership" Christ offers. The "keys" are *concepts*—biblical themes that are traceable through the Scriptures and verifiably dynamic when applied with soundly based faith under the lordship of Jesus Christ. The "partnership" is the *essential* feature of this release of divine grace;

(1) believers reaching to receive Christ's promise of "kingdom keys," (2) while choosing to believe in the Holy Spirit's readiness to actuate their unleashing, unlimited power today.

Companioned with the Bible book studies in the *Spirit-Filled Life Study Guide* series, the Kingdom Dynamic studies present a dozen different themes. This study series is an outgrowth of the Kingdom Dynamics themes included throughout the *Spirit-Filled Life Bible,* which provide a treasury of insight developed by some of today's most respected Christian leaders. From that beginning, studious writers have evolved the elaborated studies you'll pursue here.

The central goal of the subjects focused on in this present series of study guides is to relate "power points" of the Holy Spirit-filled life. Assisting you in your discoveries are a number of helpful features. Each study guide has twelve to fourteen lessons, each arranged so you can plumb the depths or skim the surface, depending upon your needs and interests. The study guides contain major lesson features, each marked by a symbol and heading for easy identification.

WORD WEALTH

The WORD WEALTH feature provides important definitions of key terms.

BEHIND THE SCENES

BEHIND THE SCENES supplies information about cultural beliefs and practices, doctrinal disputes, business trades, and the like, that illuminate Bible passages and teachings.

AT A GLANCE

The AT A GLANCE feature uses maps and charts to identify places and simplify themes or positions.

 KINGDOM EXTRA

Because this study guide focuses on a theme of the Bible, you will find a KINGDOM EXTRA feature that guides you into Bible dictionaries, Bible encyclopedias, and other resources that will enable you to glean more from the Bible's wealth on the topic if you want something extra.

 PROBING THE DEPTHS

Another feature, PROBING THE DEPTHS, will explain controversial issues raised by particular lessons and cite Bible passages and other sources to which you can turn to help you come to your own conclusions.

 FAITH ALIVE

Finally, each lesson contains a FAITH ALIVE feature. Here the focus is, So what? Given what the Bible says, what does it mean for my life? How can it impact my day-to-day needs, hurts, relationships, concerns, and whatever else is important to me? FAITH ALIVE will help you see and apply the practical relevance of God's literary gift.

As you'll see, these guides supply space for you to answer the study and life-application questions and exercises. You may, however, want to record all your answers, or just the overflow from your study or application, in a separate notebook or journal. This would be especially helpful if you think you'll dig into the KINGDOM EXTRA features. Because the exercises in this feature are optional and can be expanded as far as you want to take them, we have not allowed writing space for them in this study guide. So you may want to have a notebook or journal handy for recording your discoveries while working through to this feature's riches.

The Bible study method used in this series revolves around four basic steps: observation, interpretation, correlation, and application. Observation answers the question, What does the text say? Interpretation deals with, What does the text mean? —not with what it means to you or me, but what it meant to its original readers. Correlation asks, What light do other Scripture passages shed on this text? And application, the goal of Bible study, poses the question, How should my life change in response to the Holy Spirit's teaching of this text?

If you have used a Bible much before, you know that it comes in a variety of translations and paraphrases. Although you can use any of them with profit as you work through the *Spirit-Filled Life Kingdom Dynamics Study Guide* series, when Bible passages or words are cited, you will find they are from the New King James Version of the Bible. Using this translation with this series will make your study easier, but it's certainly not necessary.

The only resources you need to complete and apply these study guides are a heart and mind open to the Holy Spirit, a prayerful attitude, and a pencil and a Bible. Of course, you may draw upon other sources, such as commentaries, dictionaries, encyclopedias, atlases, and concordances, and you'll even find some optional exercises that will guide you into these sources. But these are extras, not necessities. These study guides are comprehensive enough to give you all you need to gain a good, basic understanding of the Bible book being covered and how you can apply its themes and counsel to your life.

A word of warning, though. By itself, Bible study will not transform your life. It will not give you power, peace, joy, comfort, hope, and a number of other gifts God longs for you to unwrap and enjoy. Through Bible study, you will grow in your understanding of the Lord, His kingdom and your place in it, and those things are essential. But you need more. You need to rely on the Holy Spirit to guide your study and your application of the Bible's truths. He, Jesus promised, was sent to teach us "all things" (John 14:26; cf. 1 Cor. 2:13). So as you use this series to guide you through Scripture, bathe your study time in prayer, asking the Spirit of God to illuminate the text, enlighten your mind, humble your will, and comfort your heart. He will never let you down.

My prayer and goal for you is that as you unlock and begin to explore God's Book for living His way, the Holy Spirit will fill every fiber of your being with the joy and power God longs to give all His children. So read on. Be diligent. Stay open and submissive to Him. You will not be disappointed. He promises you!

PART I—
The Kingdom and You

Life in the Kingdom: Foundations of the Faith illustrates how the kingdom God is both *accessible* because of Father God's gift of Jesus and *livable* because of the gift of His Holy Spirit.

"Do not fear, little flock, for it is your Father's good pleasure to give you the kingdom."

—Jesus (Luke 12:32)

As We Begin . . .

Come with me and listen to seven trumpet calls! They resound the heart and the preaching and teaching of our Lord Jesus Christ!

1. His first proclamation was, "Repent for the kingdom of heaven is at hand" (Matt. 4:17).
2. He claimed He was sent by His Father to "preach the kingdom of God" (Luke 4:43).
3. He taught His disciples to pray to their heavenly Father, "Your kingdom come, Your will be done on earth as *it is* in heaven" (Matt. 6:10).
4. He told them to "seek first the kingdom of God and His righteousness" (Matt. 6:33).
5. He promised them the kingdom belonged to "the poor in spirit" and to those who are "persecuted for righteousness' sake" (Matt. 5:3, 10).

6. He assured them that although they would be "hated by all nations for My name's sake . . . this gospel of the kingdom will be preached in all the world as a witness to all nations, and then the end will come" (Matt. 24:9, 14).

7. Further, during His last forty days before His return to heaven, He spoke to His disciples about "the things pertaining to the kingdom of God" (Acts 1:3).

Clearly the message of "the kingdom of God" was central to the teaching of Jesus. It was foundational to everything He said, everything He did and everything He came to do. What a glorious theme to call us to study!

Now, if Jesus continually spoke about the kingdom of God, *and He did,* and if the foundation of our faith is His Word, *and it is,* then how important can it be?! How important that we understand His teaching concerning "the kingdom of God"?

Life in the kingdom and the foundations of our faith are integrally related. To understand what it means to live in the kingdom of God is vital in establishing a solid foundation for our faith, especially in times like ours when the "rain and wind" Jesus forecast are increasing.

Yes, foundations are immensely important. Especially when there's a flood or an earthquake! And Jesus emphasized such significant scenarios, describing the wise and the foolish in contrast. The one built on the rock, heeding Jesus' teaching, while the other built upon the sand, rejecting it. And just as rains and wind tested where those two lived—the wise surviving and the foolish falling—so today, as rains of adverse circumstances and winds of false teaching blow, with the floods of unrighteousness rising, we need a solid foundation.

Understanding, knowing, and acting on the central core of Jesus' message as the King of the heavenly kingdom He proclaimed will stabilize and solidify more than our faith. It will secure our life and strengthen everything of our experience, our family, our business, and our witness. If the foundation of our faith is solid, we need not fear! Our house will stand on the solid foundation of the eternal Word of God.

Lesson 1/Kingdom Access

The gospel message of both John the Baptist and Jesus started with "the kingdom of God is at hand," emphasizing the nearness and availability of it and inviting hearers to come, enter, believe, repent, seek, desire it above all else, as well as to count the cost of following its King.

THE GOSPEL OF THE KINGDOM
(Mark 1:14, 15)

In contrast to Matthew and Luke, Mark does not begin his gospel with the birth of Jesus. Rather, he starts with the ministry of John the Baptist, calling it "the beginning of the gospel of Jesus Christ, the Son of God" (Mark 1:1). Apparently the "gospel" about Jesus Christ has to do, first and foremost, with the proclamation of the kingdom; thus, Mark begins the "good news" with John the Baptist and his proclamation of the kingdom rather than with the birth of the Messiah in Bethlehem. In other words, the good news of God's rule finds its focus in the final years of Jesus' life when His public ministry took place, culminating in His death, resurrection, and ascension.

The message of the "good news" has its primary focus in a Person—who He is and what He did. This Person is Jesus Christ.

Jesus' first recorded public proclamation is found in Mark 1:15 after John the Baptist's imprisonment. It consisted of two statements of fact and two imperatives for action. What were they?

First fact:

Second fact:

First imperative:

Second imperative:

 WORD WEALTH

> **Gospel,** *euangelion.* Originally used of a reward given for good news, but later is used of the good news itself. Appears seventy-seven times in the New Testament and refers to the promise of salvation and its fulfillment in the life, death, resurrection and ascension of Jesus Christ (see Mark 1:1). *Euangelion* also refers to the written narratives of Matthew, Mark, Luke, and John.

The good news of the kingdom has come near in Jesus Christ. Through Him, that which God intended from the beginning will happen: God's kingdom will come and His will will be done on earth as it is in heaven! Through His anointed Messiah-King, God will accomplish man's full redemption. This redemption will include release from sin's penalty and power, because the ransom price will be fully paid through Jesus' death on the Cross. This redemption will also include release from Satan's domination and deception, for, through death and resurrection, sin's author—Satan—will be decisively defeated. This redemption will ultimately include release from death's sting and power, for the triumph of the Son of God over death into life forevermore anticipates and guarantees ours. This is good news of the highest order! And it begins now!

ENTERING THE KINGDOM
(Matthew 18:1–5; John 3:3, 5)

Jesus offered entrance into God's kingdom now for those who would properly respond to His invitation. He made it clear that entrance into the kingdom required a right response. It is a response that requires something as different as the kingdom to be entered. Let's look again at Mark 1:15. What was the twofold response required of one who would enter God's kingdom?

WORD WEALTH

Repent, *metanoeo.* Comes from *meta* meaning "after," and *noeo,* meaning "to think," and literally means "to think afterward" in contrast to *pronoeo* which means "to think beforehand." Thus *metanoeo* is a decision that results in a change of mind leading to a change of purpose and action.

Believe, *pisteuo.* The verb form of *pistis* (faith). It includes both acceptance and adherence. When linked with the preposition *hoti* (that), *pisteuo* means "be convinced that," or "acknowledge that" something is true and to be trusted (see John 20:31). When linked with the preposition *eis* (in, into), *pisteuo* means "adhere" or "commit to" that which is trusted (see John 3:16). In reference to a person, *pisteuo* means both to accept that which is true about the individual and to commit oneself personally in light of such information. Thus, to "believe" in Jesus Christ means both to accept as true that which is said about Him and, in light of such information, to fully rely and trust Him as expressed in obedience to His words. *Pisteuo* requires both public confession *and* personal commitment.

Repent and believe the Good News! Completely turn from sin and fully trust the good news about Jesus Christ. Truly recognize Him for who He is and totally rely on Him. It seemed too simple. It was, but it was not easy. Let's turn now to Matthew 18:1–5 to see how Jesus illustrated the kind of repentance and faith required for entrance into God's kingdom. Please take note of Jesus' analogy and its point:

What is the analogy Jesus used in verse 3?

What is the point of the analogy in verse 4?

Why do you think this particular characteristic is so crucial in entering the kingdom?

In John's gospel, entering God's kingdom is described as being "born again" (John 3:3, 5). What do you think is the point of this unusual analogy?

Such passages as these make it clear that entrance into the kingdom requires a complete change from the way the world views greatness and life. So different is God's kingdom from human kingdoms that nothing less than conversion and rebirth through humble repentance and faith will gain us entrance. Good works—whether proper confession, mighty ministry, or religious position—are to no avail. All our "righteousnesses" are as filthy rags (Is. 64:6). We must experience something entirely new. We must be "born of water and the Spirit."

Thoughtfully: Even though you may have received Christ, what "new birthing" could your experience use—or does it need!—in areas where any *self*-begotten righteousness is limiting your growth?

PROBING THE DEPTHS

"Born of the Spirit" (cf. John 3:3, 5) is not difficult to explain. Scriptures are clear concerning the activity of the Holy Spirit in conversion. Read Titus 2:5, 6. What words are used for "new birth" here? Who does the work?

But, returning to John 3:5, we still must ask, "What is meant by 'born of water'? To what does 'water' refer?"

The explanations of this unusual expression are many, but most can be placed in one of three main interpretations:

1. "Water" stands for purification such as suggested by the mention of the waterpots of purification (John 2:6, 7). Thus, "water" would probably be a reference to John the Baptist's "baptism of repentance" (Mark 1:4).
2. "Water" may be connected with procreation. Since terms like "water," "rain," "dew," and "drop" were often used of male semen, "water" here could refer to natural birth in contrast to spiritual birth.
3. "Water" may refer to Christian baptism, which John's readers would have been well aware of when he wrote. However, Nicodemus would have (if this is the case) known of the water baptism that Jesus' disciples practiced (John 4:1, 2).

Further discussion of the strengths and weaknesses of each interpretation can be found in *The New International Commentary on the New Testament: the Gospel According to John* by Leon Morris (Eerdmans, 1971), pages 215–218.

DEMAND OF THE KINGDOM
(Mark 8:34–38; Luke 9:57–62; 12:8, 9; 14:25, 26)

"Repent and believe the Good News!" What wonderful news, but what demanding news! Entrance into the kingdom required a complete reorientation of values and priorities, for it was a call to life-changing discipleship.

After Peter's confession at Caesarea Philippi and Jesus' open teaching about His impending death, He began to call for a commitment to full discipleship. To believe truly that He was the Messiah, God's Son, meant to "continue in His word" as a true disciple (John 8:31). Let's take a look at what Jesus demanded. What did Jesus say a person must do if he/she would follow Him? Write down the three statements in Mark 8:34.

1.

2.

3.

Look at verses 35–38. What do you think the disciples and the multitudes understood by this call to discipleship? What was Jesus requiring of them?

 KINGDOM EXTRA

Christ's call to discipleship was demanding. It could be categorized as one of the "hard sayings" of Jesus that is not easy to fully comprehend (see F. F. Bruce's *The Hard Sayings of Jesus,* InterVarsity Press, 1983). Yet the call is clear, for the call to discipleship is embedded in the "Great Commission"—to "make disciples of all the nations" who obey all Christ has commanded (Matt. 28:19, 20). The key issue of discipleship is obedience, for without it no fundamental and lasting change takes place. This is the reason such "obedience-oriented" discipleship is required of all who would follow Christ. Otherwise, it is possible for a person to call Christ "Lord, Lord" and even do mighty works in His name and yet be an evildoer who will be denied entrance into the

eternal kingdom (Matt. 7:21–23). Initial entrance into the
kingdom of God must result in true discipleship in order to
assure ultimate entrance into God's everlasting kingdom. This
is not a matter of "salvation by works" but a matter of a
"salvation that works" (see Phil. l2:12, 13).

The demand of the kingdom was unparalleled. But so was
the price in making this blessed kingdom available. If it would
cost Jesus everything to bring God's kingdom to humankind,
could it cost people any less to enter it and enjoy its blessings?
Of course not! Thus, the demand of the kingdom required a
resolute, radical, costly, and eternal decision. Look up each
passage below and write down the illustration(s) Jesus used
and the point He was making to underscore the nature of the
decision required.

	ILLUSTRATION(S)	POINT

A resolute decision
(Luke 9:57–62)

A radical decision
(Luke 14:25, 26a)

A costly decision
(Luke 14:26b, 27)

An eternal decision
(Luke 12:8, 9)

The message of the kingdom was simple: "The time is fulfilled, and the kingdom of God is at hand. Repent, and believe in the gospel" (Mark 1:15, 16). With the coming of Jesus Christ, a time of promised fulfillment arrived. Therefore, the only appropriate response was to repent and believe this "Good News."—to turn fully from self-sufficiency and humbly trust Jesus Christ, God's Son, who died and rose to bring salvation to man.

To truly repent and believe the gospel was to be so radically transformed, it was like being "born again." It was to "enter God's kingdom." And although it required self-denial and taking up one's cross, so great was the gain that nothing must stand in the way of entering and experiencing this "Kingdom of all kingdoms"! So it is today.

THE KINGDOM REQUIRES MAN'S RESPONSE (Matthew 13:1–9, 18–23)

This truth is illustrated in one of Jesus' parables about the kingdom of God. The story is drawn from everyday life in an agrarian society. It is a story any farmer understood. Seed is scattered and falls on different kinds of soil. Thus, the result is different. The seed sown on the hardened path produced no fruit, whereas the seed sown on rocky and thorny ground produced some fruit, at least temporarily. But the seed sown on good soil produced from thirty to a hundredfold. In every case the seed sown was the same: it was the condition of the soil that determined the result. Such is the case with the kingdom of God!

With this parable we are fortunate to have Jesus' own interpretation given to His disciples in verses 18–23. Looking at these verses, answer these three questions:

1. What is the central truth, and what does it teach about God's kingdom? (Notice the frequency of the word *hear*.)

2. How does this truth differ from the popular idea of a kingdom or of independent, royal rule?

3. How should one who has "ears to hear" respond to this truth?

Although Jesus' interpretation assigned meaning to some of the details of the parable of the four soils, the main point is clear as indicated by the oft-repeated word *hear* and the concluding comment about hearing in verse 9. Write it.

This passage also explains why Jesus spoke in parables. Between this parable and its interpretation, He emphasized "unhearing" ears. Clearly the parable has a similar focus to that found in this intervening passage, namely, that people respond to the Word's teaching. In the parallel account in Mark, this theme of hearing is carried into the verses following the parable (Mark 4:23–25). Further, the understanding of the parable's point of heeding what one hears is made the key to understanding all other parables (Mark 4:13).

Thus, the condition of the soil of your heart is reflected by your willingness to hear what the Holy Spirit is seeking to communicate of Christ's life and purpose to you. The personal impact of God's sovereign kingdom power is determined by human response. God's kingdom can be rejected, temporarily accepted, or fully and fruitfully accepted. And so this pointed parable vividly pictures the varied response to Jesus' proclamation of the word of the kingdom from (a) that of the hardened scribes and Pharisees to (b) that of the temporarily responsive multitudes to (c) that of the receptive disciples.

Amazing! God's kingdom rule can be resisted or received! The same seed of the word can have such dramatically different outcomes. Like the sun, it both hardens clay and softens wax!

THE KINGDOM IS OF INESTIMABLE VALUE
(Matthew 13:44–46)

Two more parables, of the Treasure and the Pearl, focus on the value of the kingdom. A man discovers a valuable treasure hidden in a field. And what does he do? He hides it and sells all he has to buy the field! Similarly, a merchant finally finds the "pearl of great price." And what does he do? He likewise sells all he has to buy the pearl. It is important at this point to note the care that must be exercised in interpreting the details of a parable. Otherwise, one might read into these two parables the idea that the kingdom can be purchased and that, therefore, only rich people can enter it. Clearly, the Good News of the kingdom is not limited to rich people; it is for all who will "give all their heart." Now let's again answer our three questions from these two parables in Matthew 13:44–46.

1. What is the kingdom truth contained in the main point of these two parables?

2. What is different about this truth in contrast to the popular understanding of the kingdom?

3. As a "he-that-has-an-ear" person, how should you respond to this truth?

What is so new about the incalculable value of the kingdom? Would not everyone agree the kingdom is invaluable?

But notice that the kingdom is more than the costly treasure or the valuable pearl. It is like the action of the man who found the treasure and the action of a merchant who found the pearl. Its value causes people to give up everything to share in it. Thus these parables pointedly underscore Jesus' call to total and true discipleship.

FAITH ALIVE

The personal impact of God's kingdom rule is determined by an individual's response to it. Because it is God's kingdom, no kingdom is more valuable. Thus it costs one all that one has, but the sacrifice is worth it!

What do you sense the Lord may be calling you to surrender in order that broader dimensions of His kingdom might fill your life?

Lesson 2/The Kingdom's King

The best news of the kingdom is the King Himself! God is in charge. His rule is clearly seen and rightly deserved by reason of His sovereign power as Creator. Look at His "handiwork"! He made everything, and thus everything belongs to Him, including humankind, made in the image of the Creator. He deserves to rule.

But God's right to rule is most clearly and beautifully seen in His redemptive love, His "heartwork" of full salvation. Think of the King's "heartwork" in contrast with His "handiwork."

Humankind foolishly rebelled against their Creator's righteous rule. But God has mercifully sought to save people from the penalty of their sinful disobedience, that is, from spiritual death and eternal separation from Him. Thus it is that humankind rightfully belongs "twice over" to God, who has not only *made* them, but *redeemed* them. This redemption is focused in His Son who both brings and models God's sovereign rule.

In dramatic contrast to the Old Testament nation of Israel who proved to be a disobedient servant and an unfaithful witness, God seeks a kingdom of New Testament people to do His will and faithfully reflect His rule. So we now turn to a study of the Person and work of the One who came to bring that possibility and model that kingdom: the Bearer of the Kingdom—the Lord Jesus Christ, King of kings (Rev. 19:16).

JESUS AND THE KINGDOM
(Matthew 4:23–25; Acts 1:3)

If we would understand the kingdom of God, we must pay close attention to what Jesus taught and what Jesus did. Why? Look at John 14:8–11.

Matthew 4:23–25 is a summary statement of Jesus' ministry throughout Galilee and beyond. According to this passage, what did Jesus preach and what did He do?

What did Jesus preach (declaration)?

What did Jesus do (demonstration)?

What is the relationship between these two activities? Are both needed? Why?

If Jesus' entire life and ministry is a reflection and demonstration of God's kingdom, what kind of a kingdom is it? (Matt. 4:23) Why is it called "good news"?

Read Acts 1:3. What was the theme of Jesus' teaching to His disciples during His last forty days on earth?

Jesus and the kingdom are integrally related. This will become clearly evident as we come to see how Jesus Himself understood His own identity and mission. Therefore, we now look at the three titles used most frequently for Jesus in the Gospels.

JESUS, THE ROYAL "SON OF DAVID"

To understand the kingdom, we must understand the King. As we have seen, the most widely held view of the Messiah was that of a descendant of King David who would inherit his kingly rule. The Gospel of Matthew underscores this view with its opening "genealogy of Jesus Christ, the son of David, the Son of Abraham" (1:1). Now, look at Matthew 16:13–20 and 22:43–46.

Why must the Messiah be a descendant of Abraham?

Why must the Messiah be a descendant of David?

Jesus qualified at both points. Further, the frequent "that it might be fulfilled" quotations prove Jesus Christ was the Messiah promised in the Old Testament. Look up the following verses in Matthew and write down the point of fulfillment from the seven key fulfillment quotations in the first four chapters of Matthew:

1:23 (cf. Is. 7:14)

2:6 (cf. Mic. 5:2)

2:15 (cf. Hos. 11:1)

2:18 (cf. Jer. 31:15)

2:23 (cf. Is. 11:1)

3:3 (cf. Is. 40:3)

4:14–16 (cf. Is. 9:1, 2)

 PROBING THE DEPTHS

Direct quotations from the Old Testament in the New have been numbered around 250. When allusions are added, the total rises to over 600. (Some have even calculated the total to be as high as 4,000!) Such frequent use of the Old Testament in the New illustrates the understanding that the events of the life of Jesus Christ and the church reflect a period of prophetic fulfillment. The wide variation in the numbering of such usage indicates the diversity with which Old Testament passages were used by New Testament writers.

The seven fulfillment quotations above illustrate such variation. In some cases the application is quite similar to the original historical setting (Matt. 2:5 and Mic. 5:2). But in other cases, the application seems quite different from the setting in the Old Testament. For example, Hosea's reference to the Exodus of Israel as "fulfilled" in Jesus' return from Egypt is interesting (Matt. 2:15). And in still other cases one wonders what passage the writer had in mind (Matt. 2:23: "He shall be called a Nazarene"). What are we to make of all this? Misquotation? Misinterpretation? Allegorization? Spiritualization? Probably the answers are to be found in a proper understanding of the nature of "fulfillment." It does not necessarily mean "exact duplication." More likely it means practical and real "expanded application." The basic issue is the "filling full" of the original passage. Thus, the "filling full" of the Immanuel passage in Isaiah 7:14 about Jesus' virgin birth (quoted in Matt. 1:23) goes far beyond the original historical context. Just as the "filling full" of an acorn is an oak tree (not another acorn!), so the "filling full" of "God with us" is the birth of God's Son, not another human being like Isaiah's son. Classic books which have proven helpful on this question are: E. Earle Ellis's *Paul's Use of the Old Testament* (Eerdmans, 1957) and R. V. G. Tasker's *The Old Testament in the New Testament* (SCM Press, 1946).

Yes, the Gospel of Matthew clearly indicates Jesus was the Davidic Messiah. But Matthew also clearly indicates that Jesus understood His Davidic messiahship in a way different from that of the popular conception. Thus, Jesus pointedly asked His disciples not only "Who do men say that I . . . am?" but "Who do you say I am?" Read Matthew 16:13–16.

Who did men say Jesus was?

Who did the disciples say Jesus was?

Now read Matthew 16:17–20. Why do you think Jesus "commanded His disciples that they should tell no one that He was Jesus the Christ"? (*Christ* means "messiah.")

Notice both Peter's reaction to Jesus' words about His death and Jesus' response to Peter's reaction (Matt. 16:21–23). What does this indicate as to the disciples' understanding of the nature of Jesus' messiahship? Why was dying incompatible with the disciples' view of the Messiah?

To drive home the point about the true nature of His Davidic messiahship, Jesus posed a perplexing question for the Pharisees in Matthew 22:41–45. What was Jesus' point?

Yes, Jesus claimed to be the "son-of-David" Messiah, but with a difference. Jesus was a different kind of Messiah and King. He was divine, the Lord, *the* King. Therefore, His kingdom must also be different.

JESUS, THE SERVANT SON OF MAN
(Mark 10:45)

"Son of Man" was the title Jesus preferred to use of Himself. The Gospels record it on His lips over sixty-five times. Interestingly, the title is rarely, if ever, applied to Jesus by others, not even by the early church after His ascension. In fact, the only occurrence of the title outside the Gospels is in the vision of Stephen at his death (Acts 7:56). The fact that "Son of Man" appears only in Jesus' own words suggests it is a key in unlocking Jesus' own understanding of His messiahship and mission. Thus, two important questions must be answered: (a) What did Jesus' contemporaries understand by the phrase "Son of Man"? and (b) What did Jesus Himself mean by it?

There are two Old Testament uses that could have shaped popular thinking. First, there is the use in Ezekiel where God calls that prophet "son of man" over ninety times (Ezek. 2:1, 3, 6, 8, and so on). The name is unique to the prophet Ezekiel. It is usually understood as a way God was constantly reminding the prophet of the limitation and weakness of his humanity in contrast to the Lord's great power and wisdom. This seems indicated by the frequent phrase "and [then] you shall know that I *am* the Lord [*Yahweh*]" (Ezek. 6:7, 10, 14, etc.).

Second, there is the single use of the phrase "Son of Man" found in Daniel 7:13, 14. In a vision Daniel sees "One like the Son of Man" as a heavenly messianic figure who brings the kingdom of God to the suffering saints on earth. Then how did Jesus' contemporaries understand "Son of Man"? How did Jesus Himself understand it? Turn to John 12:32–34 and Luke 22:67–70 and see if you can discover the contrasting viewpoints.

Jesus' use of "Son of Man" is fascinating. Look at the first part of Mark 10:45. Why did the "Son of Man" come?

The focus of Mark's gospel is on Jesus as servant. He offers no genealogy, as Matthew and Luke do. Who wants to know the family background of a servant? In contrast to Matthew, the focus in Mark is more on Jesus' miracles than on His teaching. It is the gospel of action, for servants are better known for their deeds than for their words! And so, the "Son of Man" healed the sick, cast out demons, fed the multitudes, and raised the dead. Indeed, Jesus Christ came to serve others, not Himself.

Notice, with this, when Jesus seems to use the title "Son of Man." It seems most frequently used when He encounters misunderstanding as to who He is—especially by the unbelieving religious leaders. Look up these passages and discover what was the point of misunderstanding:

Matt. 12:32

Mark 2:10, 11

Mark 2:27, 28

Luke 7:34

Look again at Mark 10:45. Yes, the "Son of Man did not come to be served, but to serve." But for what other reason did He come, according to the last part of this verse?

Now, let's go back to Peter's confession of Jesus as Messiah in Matthew 16:13–20. Note the title Jesus used in asking who He was (v. 13). Upon Peter's answer Jesus begins to teach something He apparently had not clearly taught prior to that time. What was it? (v. 21)

 WORD WEALTH

Ransom, *lutron.* From the verb "to loose." The verb and its derivatives are used only nine times in the New Testament. The word has the idea of equivalence and is used of the price paid to release a life, such as a slave from slavery. Christ's gift of Himself was a *lutron*—"a ransom for many" (Mark 10:45). It was a sufficient price to release humankind from the sin's slavery, for it cancelled sin's debt.

This incident at Caesarea Philippi is a "hinge point" in Jesus' revelation of the true nature of His messiahship: it will involve crucifixion! From that time on, the "Son of Man" title will be connected with suffering and death. Look again at John 12:32–34. Jesus clearly tied his role as Messiah to suffering. In so doing He linked Old Testament passages which before had never been tied together—namely, Isaiah 9:6, 7 and Isaiah 52:13—53:12 passages. Look these up and consider the distinguishing differences in the role of the One being foretold.

Most significantly, the suffering "Son of Man" is to be honored with great glory. Jesus clearly taught He was the "Son of Man" who would come in power and great glory like the prophet Daniel predicted (Matt. 26:64). Thus, it appeared Jesus deliberately chose to use the title "Son of Man" to teach the true nature of His messiahship, linking suffering and ruling. Thereby, He was able to take a largely unknown title and fill it with new meaning about the true nature of His mission as Messiah. He would fulfill His messianic role through dying and rising. This would be the basis of the forgiveness of sins to be proclaimed to all nations. True deliverance from sin's tyranny required sin's penalty be paid and sin's power broken. God's kingdom rule required, first and foremost, the breaking of sin's rule. And that is why Jesus came as a suffering Servant to die and rise again.

 FAITH ALIVE

Why are suffering and death so difficult to associate with ruling and reigning? Why do we struggle with the concepts of dying in order to live, losing in order to gain, giving in order to receive? Why do we hold so tightly to what we cannot keep? Why do temporal things have such a strong hold on us? What does it take to "give up what I cannot keep to gain that which I cannot lose"? Jesus' example of exaltation through crucifixion is our pattern. Like a grain of wheat, He died. But look at the result: many seeds! Read John 12:23–26. Take some time to write your own reflections on the truth of these passages, answering the question: Am I willing to follow Jesus' example and thereby enjoy His reward?

JESUS, THE DIVINE SON OF GOD
(Luke 22:66–71; John 10:24–39)

The title "son of David" was loaded with political and economic connotations. Jewish messianic expectations held that the Messiah, David's son, would come to restore his rule. Once again the Jewish people would be free from the scourge and scorning of all foreign powers. They would control their own destiny. Therefore, although Jesus never denied he was the Davidic Messiah, He preferred to use the title "Son of Man" which did not have such popular misconceptions.

But now we study to see how His title as "Son of God" caused the most violent reactions. Let's look at Luke 22:66–71. Jesus was brought before the religious leaders by the Roman rulers. Note that all three titles were used in attempting to determine the charges against Jesus. Let's follow the dialogue:

What was the question of the religious leaders? (v. 67)

What was Jesus' two-part answer to their question? (vv. 68, 69)

a)

b)

What was the follow-up question by the religious leaders? (v. 70a)

What was Jesus' answer to their question? (v. 70b)

What did the religious leaders conclude from Jesus' answer? What had they heard from Jesus' lips that made Him worthy of death? (v. 71; cf. Matt. 26:64–66)

The debate over who Jesus really was caused no small controversy. The Romans had removed the right to implement capital punishment from the Jewish leaders, so these leaders now attempted to get the Romans to put Jesus to death by accusing Him of political insurrection against Rome as "king of the Jews." Because the Romans had the power of capital punishment and understood the serious nature of insurrection, they could be convinced that Jesus deserved to die. However, the issue that most deeply troubled the Jewish leaders was not political, but religious. To them it was blasphemy whenever Jesus claimed God as His Father. This was considered far more serious to them than insurrection against the Romans because, by making such a claim, Jesus was "making Himself equal with God" (John 5:18). No wonder they "sought all the more to kill Him"!

Little wonder Jesus tended to avoid the use of the title "Son of God" as He had done with the title "son of David" (Messiah). However, when they were applied to Him by others, Jesus never denied the application of such titles, but admitted they could be rightly used of Him. In the case of "son of David," the Jews had a wrong reaction because of a wrong interpretation. But in the case of "Son of God," they had a wrong reaction because of a right interpretation. He was the "Son of God" who was equal with the Father! He was "one" with the "Father" (John 10:30). Look at the dialogue between Jesus and the religious leaders in John 10:24–39. Carefully read the passage and write down the answers to these questions:

What question was in the leaders' minds about Jesus? (v. 24)

In response to their question, what answer did Jesus give that upset them? (vv. 30, 31)

What did *not* upset them? (vv. 32, 33)

What do you make of Jesus' answer to their charge of blasphemy in verses 34–36? What was Jesus *really* saying by quoting this passage in Psalm 82:6?

If the Jews would not believe what Jesus said about His divinity, what then should cause them to believe He was God's Son? (vv. 37–39)

Over one hundred times Jesus referred to God as "Father" in the Gospel of John. And the religious leaders knew exactly what Jesus was saying each time He called God His Father! Further, He constantly used the divine name revealed to Moses—"I AM"—to describe Himself and define His mission as God's anointed Messiah sent to accomplish redemption. Look up the following passages from John and identify what He said about Himself that applies to God alone:

6:35, 38

8:12; 9:5

8:58; 18:5, 6

10:7, 9

10:11, 14

14:7

15:1, 5

The message is clear. Jesus *is* the Son of God. In fact, that is why John wrote his gospel—that we might believe that Jesus is the Messiah, the Son of God (John 20:31). We, like Thomas, must come to the same conclusion about Jesus Christ: "My Lord and my God!" (John 20:28, 29). Only as we believe this can we have life in His name.

Indeed—HE IS THE KING!

Lesson 3/Power of the Kingdom

It is the power of the Holy Spirit that makes the kingdom "happen." "The kingdom of God *is* not in word but in power," wrote the apostle Paul (1 Cor. 4:20), noting that without the *dynamic* of the kingdom, the *word* of the kingdom contains no life-changing power. Therefore, when Paul came to Corinth it was not with "persuasive words of human wisdom, but in demonstration of the Spirit and of power" (1 Cor. 2:4, 5).

When Jesus spoke the "word" or "gospel" of the kingdom, it was always with "actualized authority." His words, like those of the apostle Paul, were always confirmed by the liberating power of the Spirit in the lives of people. Changed lives were the *fruit* of kingdom power; verifying the *force* of the word of kingdom power. As the apostle Paul put it: "Clearly *you are* an epistle of Christ, ministered by us, written not with ink but by the Spirit of the living God, not on tablets of stone but on tablets of flesh, *that is,* the heart" (2 Cor. 3:3).

The Word of God and the power of God are both essential. God's Word without the Spirit's power can result in dead orthodoxy. The Spirit without the Word can result in foolish fanaticism. But the Word and the Spirit together result in dynamic transformation. The message of the kingdom, ignited by the Spirit of God, results in dynamic kingdom ministry that genuinely liberates and profoundly transforms people. Therefore, it is essential we understand the nature, promise, reception, and release of the Spirit's power. Read Matthew 22:29. On what two points did Jesus fault the religious leaders of His day?

THE HOLY SPIRIT AND KINGDOM POWER
(Acts 1:3–8)

If you had just forty days to "wrap up" business, on what would you focus? Jesus knew His time had come to return to His Father. He had accomplished the mission for which He had been sent.

1. Crucifixion. He had done the will of the Father. "It is finished!" was His cry from the Cross as He submitted to death by crucifixion and paid the full price of humankind's redemption.
2. Resurrection. The Father had vindicated His Son's sacrifice by raising Him from the dead. Jesus then "presented Himself alive after His suffering by many infallible proofs" to His disciples.

With those two great facts—His Crucifixion and His Resurrection—in place, now see Jesus' focus. Read Acts 1:3–5 and write down the two teachings Jesus focused on with His disciples during the forty days between His resurrection and ascension:

1.

2.

These two subjects also were the focus as Jesus was about to leave and return to His Father. Look at Acts 1:6–8. Even after forty days of teaching about the kingdom of God, the disciples were still uncertain as to all it meant. What was the question they asked Jesus, and what does it reflect as to their understanding about the kingdom? (Acts 1:6)

What was Jesus' two-part answer to their question?

What was not for them to know? (Acts 1:7)

What was for them to receive? (Acts 1:8)

The Holy Spirit and the kingdom are inseparable. Powerful witness to Jesus' victory over the kingdom of darkness could only be accomplished as the Holy Spirit "came upon" the disciples. And this witness was to be their central focus, not the restoration of the kingdom to Israel which was alone the Father's business. Therefore, the coming of the Holy Spirit upon the disciples was necessary not only for powerful witness, but for proper witness, lest the disciples misrepresent the nature of the kingdom they proclaimed. The declaration of the victory of God's kingdom must be both powerfully *and* properly communicated!

THE PROMISE OF POWER
(Luke 24:48, 49)

Jesus had told His disciples not to leave Jerusalem until the "Promise of the Father" had been fulfilled in their lives (Luke 24:49). Look at Acts 1:4, 5. This promise goes back to John the Baptist (Luke 3:16). Further, Jesus Himself confirmed John's words to His disciples during His last "Upper Room Discourse" just before His death (John 14:16–18; 15:26; 16:7). Notice this promise was called the "promise of <u>the Father</u>." What is implied? Who alone is qualified to receive this "promise"? See John 14:16, 17 and Luke 11:13.

This anticipation of the Spirit goes back far beyond John the Baptist. Look at Numbers 11:24–29. What was Moses' "wish"?

Now turn to Joel 2:28, 29. What was the prophet's prophetic promise?

In the Old Testament the Spirit came upon leaders from time to time, usually giving them wisdom and prophetic powers to enable them to lead God's people. Now the promise of the Spirit is for *all* God's people. Further, the Spirit will remain *forever* and will be *in* them (John 14:16, 17). What an amazing promise . . . a universal, eternal, and internal coming of the Spirit! But also, what an essential promise! Without its fulfillment God's people would be "helpless." Notice the Spirit is called "another" Helper (John 14:16). Who, then, was the first Helper? What does this tell us about the ministry of the Holy Spirit?

WORD WEALTH

Helper, *parakletos.* A compound word from *para,* "beside," and *kaleo,* "to call"; thus the meaning of "called to one's side." The idea is one called to aid another and is used in a court of law to describe a legal assistant, counsel for the defense, an attorney, an advocate, who pleads another's cause, an intercessor. The word suggests the capability or adaptability for giving the aid required. In its widest sense *parakletos* means a helper, a comforter. It is implied that Jesus was this to His disciples when the Holy Spirit is called "another" helper (*allos,* "another of the same kind" in contrast to *heteros,* "different"). See John 14:16.

The disciples were to receive the same Spirit which Jesus Himself received at the beginning of His public ministry. They, too, were to receive the Spirit's help and power. When Jesus breathed on His disciples to receive the Holy Spirit, what did He declare? (John 20:21–23)

Thus, as Jesus' life and words faithfully witnessed to the Father by the power of the Holy Spirit, so the disciples' lives and words would bear witness to Jesus by the same power of the Holy Spirit. Not only would "another Helper" bear witness concerning Jesus *to* them, He would also bear witness *through* them to the world (John 15:26, 27). Through them both the Master and His kingdom ministry would be made known to the ends of the earth.

RECEIVING THE PROMISE
(Acts 2:1–4, 17, 18, 37–40)

The Father's promise of the Spirit was about to be fulfilled. The long-awaited gift was about to be received. The disciples obeyed the command of their Lord to "tarry in the city of Jerusalem until you are endued with power from on high" (Luke 24:49). For at least a full week, up to about 120 disciples "continued with one accord in prayer and supplication" in an upper room (Acts 1:14). Then, when "the Day of Pentecost had fully come . . . suddenly there came a sound from heaven." Read Acts 2:1–4.

What is the significance of "one accord" in verse 1? (Read *all* of Psalm 133 and note the key results of unity.)

What is suggested to your mind by the signs of windlike sound and firelike tongues in verses 2, 3? (See Ex. 3:2; 19:16–19; 1 Kin. 19:11, 12.)

What evidence do you see of promised universality in verses 1–4? (Note the words "all," "whole," "each"; also see vv. 17, 18.)

According to verse 4, what was the immediate result of the Spirit's filling? (Note what they were speaking in v. 11.)

Because the languages spoken represented up to 15 different areas of the Roman Empire, many who heard the 120 speaking recognized their "mother tongue." But those who heard languages they did not recognize assumed the speakers were drunk with wine. Peter humorously denied such was the case—it was too early in the morning, only 9:00 a.m.! Rather, "this is what was spoken by the prophet Joel," claimed the apostle Peter, quoting Joel 2:28–32. The promise of the universal outpouring of the Spirit was happening; the "last days" were here! All who called on the name of the Lord would be saved (Acts 2:21).

BEHIND THE SCENES

Jewish men were required to "appear before the LORD" in Jerusalem three times a year to celebrate the major feasts (Deut. 16:16). Passover (Feast of Unleavened Bread) in the spring celebrated Israel's deliverance from Egypt; Pentecost (Feast of Weeks), seven weeks and a day later (Greek *pentekostos* means "fifty"), celebrated first buds (firstfruits) of the barley harvest; Tabernacles (Feast of Booths) celebrated the end of the harvest in the fall. Leviticus 23 outlined the dates and duties of the annual festivals in Israel.

The analogy between the Feast of Pentecost and the outpouring of the Holy Spirit on the Day of Pentecost is seen in the "harvest" of 3,000 souls who were saved that day, becoming the "firstfruits" of a worldwide harvest. During the intertestamental period additional traditions were attached to the Feast of Pentecost. The Day of Pentecost was held to be the day on which the Law was given on Mount Sinai after Israel's deliverance from Egypt when angels transmitted the Law in the languages of the seventy nations listed in Genesis 10. It is interesting to observe that the locations from which the people came on the Day of Pentecost (Acts 2:9–11) represent approximately those areas to which the descendants of Noah's sons were scattered after the confusion of languages at the Tower of Babel. Thus, the effects of Babel were initially transcended on the Day of Pentecost when simple Galileans spoke other languages and the multitude exclaimed, "We hear them speaking in our own tongues the wonderful works of God!" (Acts 2:11).

Filled with the Holy Spirit, Peter preached the Good News about Jesus clearly, simply, and powerfully. His sermon had four points. See if you can describe each point in a sentence or two after reading Acts 2:23–36.

The historical facts about Jesus (vv. 23, 24):

Proof that Scripture predicted the Messiah's resurrection (vv. 25–32):

Proof that Scripture predicted the Messiah's exaltation with the accompanying pouring out of the Holy Spirit (vv. 33–35):

The conclusion when the story of Jesus is seen in light of fulfilled Scripture (v. 36):

Peter knew Jesus was the Messiah. He knew the Scriptures which proved it (remember those Bible studies with Jesus!); and now he also understood Jesus was not only the Messiah, He was the reigning Lord. His throne was at God's right hand, not in Jerusalem. His kingdom was a heavenly kingdom, not a kingdom of this world.

As a result of Peter's preaching, 3,000 were "cut to the heart." They were convicted by the Holy Spirit of their sin of rejecting the Messiah (John 16:7–11). And they cried out: "Men *and* brethren, what shall we do?" (Acts 2:37). Read Acts 2:38, 39 and write down the two things Peter told them to do and what would happen if they obeyed.

The first requirement:

The second requirement:

The promise to those who obey:

WORD WEALTH

Baptism, *baptisma.* From the word *bapto* meaning "to dip," signifying immersion, submersion. It is used of John the Baptist's baptism, Christian baptism, Spirit baptism, and the baptism of suffering. In each instance the totality of the person is involved.

Three thousand responded in obedience to Peter's message. They were "added" to the fellowship of 120 disciples (Acts 2:40, 41). Jesus Christ was their Lord. The community of the King had begun. Here He was "all and in all" by the power of the Holy Spirit. What traits of their life-style and discipline do you note in Acts 2:42–47? List at least five.

ANOINTING OF THE HOLY SPIRIT
(Acts 4:23–31)

The initial immersion or infilling of the Holy Spirit is a gate, not a goal. It is the beginning, not the end, of Spirit fullness. The will of the Lord is that we not be "drunk with wine in which is dissipation, but be filled [repeatedly] with the Spirit" (Eph. 5:18). In the Book of Acts those filled on the Day of Pentecost were also "refilled" subsequently. Peter, as he stood before the Sanhedrin, was "filled with the Holy Spirit" as he began his defense of teaching and preaching in the name of Jesus (Acts 4:8).

Turn to Acts 4:23–31 and read the account of a filling of an entire group of believers after the Day of Pentecost.

Why did they need to be "filled" again? (vv. 23–28)

What was their request? (vv. 29, 30)

How did the Lord answer their request? (v. 31)

Apparently repeated "fillings" or "anointings" of the Spirit are needed to meet the challenge of new and difficult circumstances. Such "anointings" are also found in the Old Testament in the lives of Samson, Saul, David and the prophets. Read the following scriptures and note the distinctive results of each "anointing."

Judg. 14:19

1 Sam. 10:10, 11

1 Sam. 16:13

1 Sam. 19:19–21

2 Chr. 15:1

2 Chr. 24:20

Ezek. 11:5

Paul, likewise, after his initial filling with the Spirit in Acts 9, was "refilled" with the Holy Spirit (Acts 13:4–12).

The kingdom of God is to be released *through* us by the power of God given *to* us. The promise of the Spirit's presence in power is given, therefore, to every child of God. From earliest times the hope had been that the Spirit would be outpoured on all flesh. At Pentecost this hope was realized and made available to every one God called to salvation.

Peter signifies the initiation of the "last days" (Acts 2:14–21 [note v. 17]), showing us the Spirit's outpouring is especially essential as we move toward the end of this age. Satan has been dealt a decisive defeat in the death and resurrection of Jesus Christ, the Lord. Knowing his "days are numbered," he makes war on the saints as they are caught up in the conflict between the kingdom of light and the kingdom of darkness (Rev. 12:10–12). Thus, they need the full armor of God to stand against the strategies of the Devil (Eph. 6:10–18). The battle is in the spiritual realm; thus, the weapons must be spiritual. Lesson 8 will explain the reason and nature of this spiritual battle and how citizens of God's kingdom can overcome the Evil One.

But it isn't just to wage and win spiritual warfare that the Holy Spirit has been given to us. The Holy Spirit helps us in many ways. One of the first and foremost is worshiping the King, an act that will pave the way for growth in every phase of kingdom living.

Lesson 4/Worship in the Kingdom

Worship is at the heart of Spirit-filled living. Jesus said, "But the hour is coming, and now is, when the true worshipers will worship the Father in spirit and truth; for the Father is seeking such to worship Him. God *is* Spirit, and those who worship Him must worship in spirit and truth." Remember how at the house of Cornelius they were heard to speak "with tongues and magnify God" (Acts 10:46). Remember at Pentecost, there were those who understood the "tongues" spoken. What did they say they heard? (Acts 2:11)

The Holy Spirit helps us worship the King. Let's think on how our worship welcomes the King's rule.

 KINGDOM EXTRA

"Establishing" God's Throne." The Psalms were the praise hymnal of the early church, and as such are laden with principles fully applicable for New Testament living today. Few principles are more essential to our understanding than this one: the <u>presence</u> of God's kingdom power is directly related to the practice of God's <u>praise.</u> The verb "enthroned" indicates that wherever God's people exalt His name, He is ready to manifest His kingdom's power in the way most appropriate to the situation, as His rule is invited to invade our setting.

It is this fact that properly leads many to conclude that in a very real way, praise prepares a specific and present place for God among His people. Some have chosen the term "establish His throne" to describe this "enthroning" of God in our midst by our worshiping and praising welcome. God awaits the prayerful and praise-filled worship of His people as an entry point for His kingdom to "come"—to enter, that His "will be done" in human circumstances. (See Luke 11:2-4 and Ps. 93:2). We do not manipulate God, but align ourselves with the great kingdom truth: His is the power, ours is the privilege (and responsibility) to welcome Him into our world—our private, present world or the circumstances of our society.[1]

WORSHIP IN SPIRIT AND TRUTH
(John 4:23, 24)

Prayer invites God's redemptive rule. Worship releases His saving reign. Perhaps the most well-known Old Testament story illustrating this truth is the story of King Jehoshaphat's victory over the Moabites and Ammonites in 2 Chronicles 20:1–30.

Faced with overwhelming odds, what did the king call the people to do? (vv. 3, 4)

What did the king (Jehoshaphat) pray? (vv. 6–12)

What happened in answer to their prayer? (vv. 14–18)

What then did the king and the people do?

vv. 18, 19

vv. 20, 21

What happened as they moved forward in battle? (vv. 22–27)

What was the long-term result of this event? (vv. 28–30)

Although such dramatic deliverance by placing praisers before the warriors is unusual in military action, the basic principle of rightly honoring the Lord as the only true sovereign over His people accounts for the victories of Israel over their enemies throughout the Old Testament. Scan Joshua 5—11; Judges 2—16; 1 Samuel 11, 17, 28—31; 2 Samuel 7—10 for examples. What general features do these examples have in common?

In Psalm 22 when David cried for help and it appeared God had forsaken him, he still acknowledged that God was "holy, enthroned in the praises of Israel," for "Our fathers trusted in You; they trusted, and You delivered them" (Ps. 22:3, 4). So the Lord would eventually deliver him, too.

A millennium later Jesus, the Messiah, the Son of David, quoted this psalm from the cross in His cry "My God!" (see Ps. 22:1). Feeling the apparent abandonment of the Father, His call was not in vain. God heard and answered, and dramatically and decisively delivered Him from death three days later. Alive forevermore! Jesus Christ now stands as the greatest and grandest example of the faithfulness of God in delivering those who rightly honor Him in total trust. Truly God *is* the Holy One who inhabits the praise and the cries of His own. Worship recognizes that this is God's essential nature and enthrones Him on the praises of His people. And in so doing, He is welcomed to increasingly further His saving and delivering work!

ACCEPTABLE WORSHIP
(Hebrews 12:28, 29; 13:15, 16)

The writer of Hebrews wisely exhorts us that, "since we are receiving a kingdom which cannot be shaken, let us have grace, by which we may serve God acceptably" (Heb. 12:28). How amazing! What God requires, He gives as a gift. His amazing grace graciously gives to us the required righteousness of Christ for entrance into His eternal kingdom, and graciously gives to us the required grace to serve/worship Him acceptably. Look up Hebrews 12:28, 29.

How is "acceptable worship" defined? (v. 28)

Why is such "acceptable worship" essential? (v. 29)

Now let's look at Hebrews 13:15, 16 and identify the two kinds of "sacrifices" that are to be included in "acceptable worship [service]" to God. What are they?

v. 15

v. 16

In the New Testament the clearest teaching about the saving nature of worship is found in Jesus' dialogue with the woman at the well in John 4. When asked what appeared to be an evasive question about where to worship, Jesus turned the woman's inquiry into an opportunity to teach about true worship. Look what Jesus said:

What is more important—where we worship or whom we worship? Why? (vv. 21, 22)

What is God the Father seeking? Why? (v. 23)

How must true worshipers worship God the Father? Why? (vv. 23, 24)

True worship reflects the nature of the God we worship. Only by the Spirit of truth can we worship "in spirit and in truth." God's Spirit enables us to rightly worship Him according to who He is—spirit and truth. Worship by the Spirit of God according to the truth of God as revealed by the Son of God is the kind of worship the Father seeks. Such worship exalts God as Father, the source and sovereign of all things who has sent His Son to do His will and finish His redemptive work as the Savior of the world (see John 4:34, 42). When the Spirit was outpoured on the Day of Pentecost, the immediate consequence was praise to God for His "wonderful works" of redemption through His Son, Jesus Christ (Acts 2:11). And such praise prepared the way for God's saving rule to be proclaimed and experienced in the lives of 3,000 people who put their full trust in the crucified Christ as the reigning Messiah and Lord.

 FAITH ALIVE

Some would focus on the spirit of worship and encourage freedom of expression in praise. Others would focus on the truth of worship and encourage soundness of understanding in adoration.

We may enter in with *both*—according to the Scriptures. Read Psalm 100 and note which expressions would be more open, and which more pensive.

1. Outward expression:

2. Inward thoughtfulness

UNIVERSAL WORSHIP: GOD IS KING
(Psalm 47:1–9; 145:10–13)

All peoples are called to clap and shout praise to God because "He is a great King over all the earth" (Ps. 47:1, 2). They are to "sing praises with understanding" (Ps. 47:7). Look at Psalm 47:8, 9 and discover what such "understanding" includes. Write down the reasons given for praising God as King of all the earth:

WORD WEALTH

Clap, *taqa'.* To clatter, clang, sound, blow (trumpets), clap, strike. This verb occurs more than 65 times. "Strike" may be the truest one-word definition; "sound" is also a possibility. *Taqa'* describes pitching a tent or fastening a nail, probably due to the striking of the hammer used for both tasks. In other references, *taqa'* describes blowing a trumpet or sounding an alarm. Thus *taqa'* indicates energy and enthusiasm. Here all nations are commanded to clap their hands and shout triumphantly to God. Formalistic religion seeks to discourage this kind of worship, although God has built into the human being an almost instinctive urge to clap and shout when victory is experienced.[2]

Worship has to do with rulership. Kings are honored for their authority to rule. But God alone is King over all the earth. He alone is the ultimate Ruler from whom all earthly kings derive their ruling authority (Rom. 13:1). He alone "puts down one, and exalts another" (Ps. 75:7). Therefore, universal worship is due His name. He alone is King of kings, yet His rule is a benevolent rule. King David understood this. What does he say in Psalm 145:9?

In response, what did David declare? (v. 10)

What do the saints speak of in their blessing of God? (v. 11)

What is the result of such blessing of God? (v. 12)

What is the nature of God's kingdom? (v. 13)

 FAITH ALIVE

Good theology is doxology. To know God in truth is to worship Him truly. When we see what the psalmists saw, we will do what the psalmists did . . . sing praises with understanding! Our understanding of God is the foundation of our worship of God and allows His right to rule as Savior and Deliverer of His people.

KINGDOM EXTRA

Sing Praises with Understanding. The word "understanding" (Hebrew *sakal,* "prudent or cautious, and hence, intelligent") is linked to wisdom and prosperity. Proverbs 21:16 provides contrast to such understanding: "A man who wanders from the way of understanding will rest in the assembly of the dead." But when we "sing praises with understanding," we are giving testimony to God's love for us and our love for Him. Life results instead of death. Others, listening to us praise God, hear testimony of our salvation and our joyful relationship with Him, which often leads to their own salvation.[3]

If God is infinite and His kingdom eternal, we shall never run out of reasons to praise Him. As our understanding of Him increases, so will our worship of Him. Even within the finite world in which we live we have come to understand God through His Word and His Spirit.

On occasion, the psalmists would make use of acrostic (alphabetical) poems to express their prayer and praise to God (Ps. 10; 25; 34; 111; 112; 119; 145). Starting with the first letter in the Hebrew alphabet, they would begin a line, couplet, or stanza with each successive letter. Although not every acrostic psalm was complete with all twenty-two Hebrew letters employed, the beauty and power of the poem was evident. Why not attempt your own "modified version" of an acrostic poem of praise in your own language? Beginning with the first letter of the alphabet, try naming an attribute or characteristic of God revealed in Scripture for each letter.

A_____   B_____   C_____

D_____   E_____   F _____
and so on.

Now, for the next thirty days, why not begin to use this acrostic as the basis of singing or speaking "praise with understanding" to God. Let your theology turn into a doxology of praise to the One who is your sovereign Creator and loving Savior, the King of all the earth!

As we focus our worship and attention on our King, "the author and finisher of *our* faith," (Heb. 12:1), we can expect people around us to see Him in the way we live.

As children of the King, we are kingdom people, and His genes are in us to make us conformable to His character. Write out 1 Peter 1:23.

Of course, as you would suspect, the kingdom takes on the character of its King. Write this truth as expressed in Colossians 1:13.

Now, let's pursue these graces of transformation!

1. *Spirit-Filled Life Bible* (Nashville, TN: Thomas Nelson Publishers, 1991), 770–771, "Kingdom Dynamics: 'Establishing' God's Throne."

2. Ibid., 794, "Word Wealth, 47:1 clap."

3. Ibid., 795, "Kingdom Dynamics: Sing Praises with Understanding."

Lesson 5/Kingdom Living

God's kingdom is so different, it can be overlooked by those uninterested. It is like insignificant leaven and mustard seed. Its size can be misleading. Based on outward appearance it may seem ordinary and mundane. But based on its essential character, no kingdom is more significant than God's kingdom. It has unparalleled transforming power.

Not only do people enter the kingdom, the kingdom enters them! The kingdom does not consist of "eating and drinking, but righteousness and peace and joy in the Holy Spirit" (Rom. 14:17). Look up each of those words and distill their key meaning as this passage is relating it.

Righteousness

Peace

Joy (in the Holy Spirit)

The kingdom of God consists of transformed people. They think differently, they see differently, they hear differently, they act differently. In a word, they live differently. Why? Because they *are* different!

When we have truly repented of self-focused living and have fully believed the good news of Jesus Christ, we will "live no longer for themselves, but for Him who died for them and rose again" (2 Cor. 5:15). The King of the kingdom is our

Lord. We are "in Him," and He is in us. Therefore we are "a new creation: old things have passed away; behold, all things have become new" (2 Cor. 5:17).

Jesus has called us as His followers to self-denying discipleship, to a process of profound transformation. As citizens of God's kingdom, disciples of Jesus Christ increasingly are to reflect the character of the One under whose authority they have come and within whose kingdom they live. The character of the King and His kingdom becomes their character. What does 2 Peter 1:4 say we will begin to "partake" of?

This lesson will examine several of these identifying characteristics of those who are becoming "partakers" as sons of the kingdom.

SONS OF THE KINGDOM
(Matthew 8:11, 12)

Only entrance into God's kingdom gives one the right to be called a "son of the kingdom." The scribes and Pharisees were self-deceived. Like the prodigal son's elder brother, they saw no need of repentance, for they believed they were already "righteous." They thought they were already "sons of the kingdom." But their cynical and jealous response to Jesus' eating with "sinners" invalidated their claim. If they were truly "sons of God's kingdom" they would, like their heavenly Father, rejoice over lost "sinners" returning to His family. Read Luke 15:11–32. Contrast the father's attitude toward the returning son with the boy's older brother's.

Let's look at Matthew 8:11, 12 and see what Jesus said about these so-called "sons of the kingdom." Notice the context of these verses in Matthew 8:5–13. What is the distinguishing characteristic of a true "son of the kingdom"? (v. 10; cf. Heb. 11:6)

What did the Gentile Roman centurion see in Jesus that so many Israelites missed? (vv. 8, 9)

What will happen to the person who does not have this "distinguishing characteristic"? (v. 12) What does this mean?

"Insiders" thrown out and "outsiders" invited into the kingdom! Clearly the kingdom of God is not to be confused with any other kingdom, including the kingdom of Israel. Religious heritage and ritual is not to be confused with spiritual regeneration and rebirth. "Sons of the kingdom" are those whom the Father has delivered "from the power of darkness and conveyed . . . into the kingdom of the Son of His love" (Col. 1:13). They are those whom the Father has qualified "to be partakers of the inheritance of the saints in the light" (Col. 1:12). By their fruit you will know them, and such evidence of divine life described by the apostle Paul as the "fruits of righteousness which *are* by Jesus Christ to the glory and praise of God" (Phil. 1:11).

RIGHTEOUSNESS IN THE KINGDOM
(Matthew 5:17–48)

The "Sermon on the Mount" is for "sons of the kingdom." What Jesus taught was for His disciples who had "ears to hear" (Matt. 5:1, 2). Therefore, this "sermon" is *not* a set of noble ethics for an ideal religious society. Nor is it a prescription for successful living based on this world's philosophies. Rather, the "Sermon on the Mount" is a description of *God's* standard of righteousness characterizing the citizens of *His* kingdom. And it stands in stark contrast to the self-centered, prideful, unchildlike religious righteousness of the scribes and Pharisees, which was artificial, external, legalistic, and burdensome. Let's look how Jesus compared such "righteousness" with the true righteousness of God's kingdom. Write down the six contrasts He gives in Matthew 5:

Matthew 5	RELIGIOUS RIGHTEOUSNESS (keeps the "letter of the Law")	KINGDOM RIGHTEOUSNESS (fulfills the "spirit of the Law")
vv. 21–26		
vv. 27–30		
vv. 31, 32		
vv. 33–37		
vv. 38–42		
vv. 43–48		

What does such religious righteousness add up to? What does such kingdom righteousness add up to? Turn to Galatians 5:19–25 and write down the apostle Paul's conclusions (note especially the end of verse 21 and all of verse 22).

 WORD WEALTH

Righteousness, *dikaiosune.* The quality of being right or just. When used of God, it refers to His faithfulness, truthfulness, justice, and rightness consistent with His own nature and promises. God's *dikaiosune* is seen most dramatically and clearly in the death of Christ (Rom. 3:25, 26). When used of man, it means conformity to the revealed standards and will of God. *Dikaiosune* is both a legal and gracious term. It sets forth the legal standards of judgment upon which a person is declared guilty or not guilty. Although all have sinned and are declared guilty, God graciously declares repentant sinners not guilty and imparts His righteousness to them because of Christ's righteous life and atoning death on the Cross.

Kingdom righteousness is the righteousness that "exceeds" that of the most religious person, for it is an inward righteousness of a heart where the King reigns. It is not an external observance of rules and regulations, but an expression of the internal reality of a relationship with God through Jesus Christ who is Lord.

SPIRIT OF THE KINGDOM
(Matthew 18:21–35)

Perhaps one of the most unique and amazing characteristics of God is that He is a forgiving God. Listen to the words of the prophet Micah: "Who is a God like You, pardoning iniquity and passing over the transgression . . . He delights in mercy . . . [and] will cast all our sins into the depths of the sea" (Mic. 7:18, 19). We saw how the parable of the Prodigal Son reveals the forgiving heart of God our Father. Such a spirit of forgiveness is, therefore, to characterize His children. So important is this matter of forgiveness, that of all the statements in the Lord's Prayer, it alone is amplified at the conclusion of the prayer (Matt. 6:14, 15).

This spirit of forgiveness is the focus of a very pointed parable Jesus taught His disciples in response to a practical question by Peter. What was the question he asked? (Matt. 18:21)

Look at the verses just before verse 21 (Matt. 18:15–20). What is the context of the question on forgiveness?

How did Jesus answer Peter's question? (v. 22)

Do you think "seventy times seven" is to be taken literally? What do you think Jesus meant, exactly?

Now let's look at the parable that explains forgiveness in the kingdom of heaven (Matt. 18:23–35). For some unexplained reason, a servant owed his master a sum of money so large it could never be repaid, even if he and his family were sold to make payment. Yet he pleaded: "Master, have patience with me, and I will repay you <u>all</u>" (v. 26). The master was moved by compassion with his plea and forgave him the entire debt. Freed from his unpayable debt, the servant found a fellow servant who owed him a mere one hundred days' wages, a very small debt in comparison to the debt he had been forgiven. He demanded full and immediate payment, for now the money would be his, since the huge debt he owed was cancelled. The fellow servant could not pay and made the same plea for mercy as he had. But instead of showing mercy and forgiving the debt, which was surely payable given enough time, he threw his fellow servant into prison until he paid all. When the other servants saw what he did, they told the master. The master was so angry he delivered him to the "torturers" (not simply to prison, but to punishment) until full payment was made. Why? Because he had not treated his fellow servant as he had been treated! What's the point? See verse 35!

Now let's ask ourselves the same three questions we asked of the kingdom parables in Lesson 7:

What is the main point of the parable, and what kingdom truth is found within it? (Note the phrase "from his heart" in v. 35.)

How does this kingdom truth differ from popular understanding?

What should a disciple who has ears to hear do about this truth?

✎ WORD WEALTH

Forgive, *aphiemi.* To send away, to remit, completely cancel. In reference to the sinner it signifies the remission of punishment, the cancelling of sin's penalty or debt.

Charizomai is the noun used of the act of forgiveness in which unconditional favor and kindness is freely and mercifully shown. The word is from the same root as the word for "grace" *(charis).*

On this crucial theme, Jack Hayford has written a brief article which appears in the *Spirit-Filled Life Bible:* "Kingdom Dynamics: Forgiveness" (Thomas Nelson, 1991), pages 1440–1441.

Forgiveness from the heart does not keep a score of wrongs. It "remembers to forget"! True forgiveness is a spirit, not a statistic. Who could keep track of 490 offenses by a brother? Heart forgiveness is like God's forgiveness—it is always available when needed. Surely such a spirit of forgiveness must come from the Spirit of God. Clearly, "to err [sin] is human, but to forgive is divine." Thus, forgiveness, unlimited and heartfelt, can only come from God Himself . . . and it has in Christ! And so we are commanded to treat others as we have been treated. We are to "be kind to one another, tenderhearted, forgiving one another, even as God in Christ forgave you" (Eph. 4:32).

 FAITH ALIVE

No experience transcends that of forgiveness. God completely "let it go" when in His great mercy He cancelled the entire debt our sins had incurred. Amazing grace! Why, then, do we find it so difficult to "let it go" when a brother or sister offends us? Could it be we have not really understood the size and significance of the debt God in Christ forgave us? Sometimes we are halfhearted in forgiving those who have sinned against us. We say; "I'll forgive, but I won't forget!" But that is forgiving from the head, not from the heart! What if God forgave us like that? True forgiveness: "lets it go" completely . . . no digging up of the past. "But you don't know how deeply I've been hurt!" we cry. Hurt more deeply than Jesus was by our sins? If He can forgive, so can we. Further, in giving forgiveness we are simply giving what we have already received—His forgiveness!

"Let it go" and let healing come both to you and to the one you forgive. It is essential for your health, as well as for their health—spiritually, emotionally and physically.

It's important to stress that forgiveness is a process and may not always be accomplished in the blink of an eye. After we have forgiven all offenses and hurts we are conscious of, God may reveal a deeper level of pain, as we are emotionally able to handle it, in order to lead us to complete freedom—one step at a time. The point is that we must 1) choose to begin the forgiveness process and 2) respond immediately to those new areas of pain that the Lord may surface through time. Then, as we continue to "give it up" to Jesus, its power over our memories will gradually be released until we are no longer tormented by those painful memories of our past experience.

GREATNESS IN THE KINGDOM
(Mark 10:35–45; Luke 22:24–30)

On several occasions Jesus' disciples argued about who was the greatest. James's and John's request through their mother to sit at honored positions in the kingdom upset the other disciples, who probably thought they were better qualified for such important positions (Mark 10:35–41). Again, a dispute broke out among the disciples at the Last Supper, just before Christ's crucifixion, about who should be considered the greatest.

In both instances Jesus used Himself as an example of one who came to serve. Note the dramatic contrast between "rulers over the Gentiles" and servants in the kingdom as illustrated by Jesus Himself who came to serve and not be served. Read Mark 10:42–45 and write out a definition of:

Greatness in this world's kingdoms:

Greatness in God's kingdom:

Look at Luke 22:27. Who is greater? He who sits at the table or he who serves? Why?

Jesus pointed to Himself as being one among the disciples who served. He then gave them a living example of true greatness as He began to do something unheard of for an honored guest at a meal—He washed the disciples' feet! Let's read John 13:1–17 and discover what happened, why, and what we are to learn from this fascinating story.

Why the need for verse 3 to introduce the footwashing?

What happened with Peter? (vv. 7–9)

Why did Peter react like this?

What is the point of the "bathing vs. footwashing" analogy in verses 10 and 11?

What was the point of the footwashing? (vv. 14, 15)

What did Jesus mean when He said: "If you know these things, blessed are you if you do them"? (v. 17)

REWARD IN THE KINGDOM
(Matthew 20:1–16)

The treatment of the workers in the vineyard by the landowner in the kingdom parable found in Matthew 20:1–16 pointedly illustrates how different is the kingdom of God from men's kingdoms. Again, the story is a familiar one. Day laborers standing idle waiting for work was common then and now. Some were hired for an agreed-upon price early in the morning, while others were hired for a fair price at 9:00 A.M., Noon, and 3:00 P.M. But some were also hired for a fair price at 5:00 P.M. When the day's work was over, the workers were given their wages by the landowner beginning with those who were hired last. Amazingly, the 5:00 P.M. workers received the same amount as those who were hired early in the morning. Of course, the workers who had "borne the . . . heat of the day" complained that the landowner was unfair! But was he? Had he not paid these day-long workers the amount he had promised them? In fact, did he not do the same with all the workers? So what's the point? What are we to make of this rather surprising parable? Again, let's ask ourselves these questions:

What is the parable's point, and what kingdom truth is found within it?

How does this truth about God's kingdom differ from the popular understanding?

How should a disciple who is willing to hear such truth respond?

How great and gracious is the reward for those who have ears to hear and hearts to respond—a hundredfold in this life and eternal life hereafter when those who seemed to have been "first" in this life will be "last," and those who appeared to be "last" will be "first" (Matt. 19:29, 30)!

"Sons of the kingdom" live in dramatic contrast to "sons of the wicked one." Both reflect the characteristics of their fathers. "Sons of God's kingdom" reflect their Father's righteousness, forgiveness, and servanthood. "Sons of the wicked one's kingdom" reflect their father's unrighteousness, unforgiveness, and dominating spirit. "Sons of the kingdom" live in a family where their Father graciously rewards them not according to their merits, but according to His! "Sons of the wicked one" live in a family where their father deceives and eventually destroys his own children.

In His life and ministry Jesus Christ, God's eternal Son, perfectly revealed the character of His Father and the nature of His kingdom in righteousness, forgiveness, and servanthood. In Him God's kingdom has come, and His will has been done on earth as it is in heaven. Through His death and resurrection He has graciously provided all that is needed for life and godliness. He now invites all who have an ear to hear and a heart to obey not only to reflect the kingdom's character, but to experience the kingdom's ministry.

Lesson 6/Prayer and the Kingdom

Although the kingdom is under God's sovereign authority and, like a seed, grows of itself, God has invited His people to partner with Him in establishing and advancing His kingdom in this age. As we have said, "Prayer invites God's rule; worship releases His reign." By this we note with discernment the place God has given us under His sovereign rule. "Without prayer," John Wesley said, "God will do nothing." Our prayer, praise and worship are *mighty* under God, to invite His kingdom into our affairs and the affairs of this world. What an awesome privilege and responsibility to be colaborers with God in furthering His redemption purposes on planet earth!

Such a high and holy calling is based on relationship with God as Father. The rights and responsibilities of family come with new birth into the household of faith. Read the words of the apostle Paul in Romans 8:15–17.

Now, notice how the passage continues. Because the promised kingdom of righteousness has come in Jesus Christ, there is now a "groaning" and a yearning as we await the full revelation of God's rule in the age to come. Please write down the three "groanings" found in this passage (vv. 22, 23, and 26).

1.

2.

3.

- Worship sees things as they should be—God rightfully honored as Sovereign Creator and Redeeming Savior. He alone is worthy to be so praised, adored, honored, and exalted.
- Prayer sees things as they are—man wrongfully usurping God's rule, violating His Law, and destroying His creation. Prayer believes and insists this must change.

Thus, prayer becomes an expression of the deep-seated desire and groaning to see wrongs righted, sin abolished, death destroyed, and the curse removed—to see God's kingdom come and His will be done on earth as it is in heaven.

So now, let us explore the nature and power of prayer in establishing and extending the sovereign and redemptive rule of God in this *present* age in preparation for the glorious age to come.

YOUR KINGDOM COME!
(Matthew 6:9–15)

Few passages of Scripture are better known than what is called "The Lord's Prayer." Several key questions will focus for us the nature and power of this "Disciples' Prayer" given by Jesus to people who have truly committed themselves to the King and His kingdom. The prayer appears in Matthew 6:9–15 (Luke 11:2–4 is a shortened form). Read carefully the prayer in both places, and seek to answer these questions:

This prayer is given as a contrast to other kinds of praying. What is the major difference between them? (Matt. 6:5–8)

Note that the prayer is divided into two major parts. What is the focus of the first part in verses 9 and 10? What is the focus of the second part in verses 11–13? (Compare this twofold focus with Jesus' words in Matt. 22:37–40.)

The prayer begins with "Our Father." What is the significance of the word *our*? What is the significance of the word *Father*?

Write down the first three requests of the prayer found in verses 9 and 10.

1.

2.

3.

Write down the next three requests of the prayer found in verses 11–13.

1.

2.

3.

Which of these requests is amplified in verses 14 and 15? Why?

Note how the prayer ends in the last part of verse 13. Why the word *for.* What is the connection of this ending and the previous requests?

    FAITH ALIVE

All religions pray, but not all pray properly. Jesus' instruction on how to pray came out of His own prayer life, when His disciples, having observed Him praying, asked Him to "teach us to pray" (Luke 11:1). In Matthew Jesus made clear that the way He taught His disciples to pray is in dramatic contrast to the praying of both the hypocrites who pray for public acclaim and the heathen who pray with meaningless repetition (Matt. 6:5–8). Jesus' own relationship with His Father was the basis of His effective prayer life and must be likewise for His followers. If, like Jesus, they seek first God's kingdom and righteousness, their heavenly Father will also take care of their essential needs (Matt. 6:33). This principle of priority is clear in the prayer Jesus gave His disciples. God's concerns come first, our needs second. And the force of this priority is seen most clearly in the word order and the verbal form used in each of the first three requests related to God's concerns. The verb appears first and is in the imperative mood, which underscores an insistent demand, not merely a wishful desire. The three Godward requests literally translate as follows:

"Let it be hallowed . . . Your name!"
"Let it come . . . Your kingdom!"
"Let it come about . . . Your will!"

Prayer, Jesus' style, reflects a greater concern for God's interests than for our interests. And as a result, our interests are most certainly cared for! Further, our interests are the Father's interests even before we are aware of them (Matt. 5:8)! Thus, prayer becomes conversation between two people who have each other's interests at heart and give them highest priority! No wonder we need not pray to get anyone's attention—men's or God's. Men's we do not need, and we already have God's attention. He knows what we need—He is our Father! Thus, we do well to give priority to His honor, kingdom, and will when we pray daily for provision, pardon, and protection. Ask the Holy Spirit to make you consistently aware of God's concerns whenever you pray about yours. What does Matthew 6:33 promise to such a seeker?

PERSISTENTLY RESISTING THE STATUS QUO
(Luke 18:1–8)

The "Lord's Prayer" helps us understand the nature of prayer. It is an invitation to ask and receive daily from our heavenly Father physical provision, forgiveness and spiritual protection. He knows what we need even before we ask. But it is in the larger context of God's honor, kingdom, and will that the receiving of such personal answers take on their true significance. He invites us to partner with His desires as we seek the answers to our own. As He has made meeting our daily needs His priority, He asks that we make seeking His kingdom and righteousness our priority. In so doing we make possible not only the fulfilling of our personal needs, but the accomplishing of His redemptive purposes. Thus, in anticipation of the final consummation of God's kingdom and His saving purposes, we ask that His name be honored today in this world. As His children we request that this happen by His kingdom coming and His will being done on earth as it is in heaven.

As we patiently long for the full manifestation of God's righteous rule on earth at the end of this age, we faithfully persist in resisting the "status quo" in this age. Through prayer we insist that what "is" must come under the "ought" of God's kingdom . . . today! Jesus Himself taught us to do so! Look at His parable about the persistent widow in Luke 18:1–8.

What is the point of the parable, and what is the truth taught about God's kingdom?

In what way, if any, does this truth differ from common perceptions?

In light of this truth, what personal application is called for on my part?

WORD WEALTH

Avenge, *ekdikeo.* From *ek,* "out," and *dike,* "justice," meaning that which proceeds from justice and has to do with vindicating a person's right or righting a wrong. The verb *ekdikeo* appears six times in the New Testament and is used of the vindication of the rights of a widow (Luke 18:3, 5) and God's avenging of the blood of the martyrs (Rev. 12:6; 19:2). The noun *ekdikos* is used twice, of civil authorities who exact a penalty from a wrongdoer (Rom. 13:4) and of the Lord who does likewise with one who wrongs his brother, especially in the matter of adultery (1 Thess. 4:6). The noun *ekdikesis,* "vengeance," is found nine times and is used in three passages with the verb *poieo,* "to make," and thus means "avenge" (Luke 18:7, 8; Acts 7:24). Twice *ekdikesis* is used in a statement that "vengeance" belongs to the Lord (Rom. 12:19; Heb. 10:30). In 2 Thessalonians 1:8 it is God who rightly exacts justice, without vindictiveness, upon those "who do not know God, and . . . do not obey the gospel of our Lord Jesus Christ."

The story of the unjust judge underscores God's willingness to hear the prayers of His chosen ones who persistently cry out to Him to right life's wrongs and see the righteous rule of God replace the rule of evil men. It is a passionate cry to see "His kingdom come and His will be done on earth as it is in heaven." Such intercessory prayer flourishes where there is: 1) a sincere concern that God's name is hallowed too irregularly, His kingdom has come too infrequently, and His will is done too inconsistently; and 2) a confident assurance God can do something about it. Jesus' own example vividly illustrates this kind of faith. His consistent and persistent praying clearly indicated He refused to live in this world or do His Father's will on any terms other than His Father's. In a word, He rebelled against the status quo of a world in its fallen and perverse abnormality. We are to do likewise.

 FAITH ALIVE

Why do we give up so quickly? Why do we faint in prayer so readily? Is it not because we really do not believe it will make a difference? Thus we accept, perhaps unwillingly, the situation as unchangeable. And that's the point of the story of the poor widow and the unjust judge. She could not stop insisting on justice, because she believed it would make a difference . . . and it did! She prayed . . . until the situation changed.

How much more will such continuance with God bring results! He is no wicked judge. He is the One who has invited us as His chosen ones to ask His kingdom to come and His will to be done.

Where do you see God's honor, rule, and will not being acknowledged and honored?

Have you wearied of praying? The parable is for you. You *will* reap in due season if you faint not.

HOUSE OF PRAYER FOR ALL NATIONS
(Mark 11:15–18; 1 Timothy 2:1–6; Revelation 5:6–10)

The nature and power of prayer in petitioning our heavenly Father to accomplish His will and purpose on earth is indeed an awesome and amazing reality. It is an awesome reality because God invites us to partner in the fulfillment of

His redemptive purposes on earth. It is an amazing reality because it works! Oh, the unfathomable wisdom and mercy of our Sovereign Creator and Redeeming Savior! And although the biblical "now, not yet" tension requires us to humbly acknowledge there is a God-ordained limit as to the full coming of His kingdom on earth now, there is no such limit as to whom God wants the initial blessings of His kingdom to come before this age ends. He wants people of "all nations" to experience the benefits of His transforming rule through the Good News of the gospel of Jesus Christ.

Jesus' reflection of the Father's compassion for all "nations" is seen in His response to the merchandising of the moneychangers in the temple courts in Mark 11:15–18. Why did Jesus get so upset and drive out those who bought and sold in the temple court of the Gentiles? What is the significance of the two statements made in verse 17? Look up the Old Testament context of the quotation from Isaiah 56:7 for the first statement and Jeremiah 7:11 for the second statement.

First statement:

Second statement:

Further, look at the immediate context of this cleansing of the temple in Mark 11. It is the story of the cursing of the barren fig tree, a symbol of national Israel's lack of the fruit of repentance. The universal witness of God through His ancient people, Israel, was coming to an end. Instead of being a "house of prayer for all nations," the temple had become a "den of thieves"!

God's dwelling place in Jerusalem would be destroyed in A.D. 70. Still, God's gracious intention toward all humankind remained intact. Turn to 1 Timothy 2:1–6 to see what the apostle Paul said about the priority of prayer among God's people.

For whom are we to pray with thanksgiving? (vv. 1, 2a)

Why are we to pray like this for such people? What are the results? (v. 2b)

Why are such results "good and acceptable in the sight of God"? What is His desire? (vv. 3, 4; cf. 1 Tim. 4:9, 10)

Whom has God provided as a "ransom" so this can happen? (vv. 5, 6)

Prayer and resisting the status quo are connected with world evangelization. What are we further taught about prayer and God's purpose for the spread of the gospel? Note what each passage below says:

Eph. 5:18, 19

Col. 4:2–4

2 Pet. 3:9

Our intercession for all nations is to be a reflection of God's desire that none perish. Therefore, our gathering places should be characterized by "prayer for all nations" and the "presence of all nations" as God opens the door of salvation to them in answer to our faithful and compassionate petitions.

Again, the connection between prayer and world evangelization is seen in Revelation 5:6–10. John's heavenly

vision revealed that the Lion who triumphed is a slain Lamb.
He alone is the One qualified to open the seven-sealed scroll in
God's right hand. Note the two items the elders have with
which to honor the Lamb. What are they, and what do they
represent? (v. 8)

In some manner the prayers of the saints are vitally
connected with the song of universal redemption which
follows. Look at the message of the "new song" addressed to
the Lamb in verses 9 and 10.

Why is the Lamb worthy to open the seals? (v. 9a)

Who was included in the Lamb's redemption? (v. 9b)

What are the redeemed called, and what is their mission?
(v. 10)

Again, in Revelation 8:3, 4 the rising incense with "the
prayers of all the saints" ascended before God. Apparently in
some manner they prepare the way for the dramatic and cli-
mactic consummation of God's judgments on earth in the
seven trumpets and seven bowls (Rev. 8—16). Even in the
outpouring of these final righteous judgments upon the
wicked there is divine mercy, for they are designed to bring
humankind to repentance and worship of the true and living
God before it is too late (Rev. 9:20, 21). Yes, the coming of
God's kingdom both within and at the end of history is
accompanied by the "prayers of the saints." They seek an end
to the status quo of a world turned upside down in rebellion
against its Creator and a righting of the wrongs which insult
His holy and righteous name. They begin and sustain the work
of the kingdom.

Lesson 7/Ministry of the Kingdom

When Jesus came announcing, "Repent, for the kingdom of heaven is at hand," He had one goal—that the Father's will might be done! The presence of the Father's rule through His ministry was to overthrow evil. He was the initial *Release* of the redemption of God. He came as King to release humankind from the bondage of self, sin, sickness, and Satan. He came as a *Restorer* to restore relationship with God, to restore what man lost in the Fall; to lay the foundation through His Cross for the release of all other blessings.

What did the angel say to Joseph about Jesus' purpose? (Matt. 1:20, 21)

How did the announcement of the angel to the shepherds at the birth of Jesus confirm this? (Luke 2:10, 11)

God is a saving God. Describe the content of these two verses as they show what Jesus' foundational ministry was to provide:

Luke 19:10

1 Tim. 2:4–6

Therefore, the foundational ministry of the kingdom is the ministry of salvation. But within salvation's full provision are deliverance, release, and liberation from all that prevents God's will from being accomplished. The coming of the kingdom is to bring about the fulfillment of God's saving purposes for humankind, that they might live "to the praise of His glory" (Eph. 1:12). Let's study how the saving ministry of the kingdom in the life of our Savior, Jesus Christ, is overflowing with love and grace to bring praise and glory to God through His manifest works in us.

    WORD WEALTH

Salvation, *soteria.* Rescue, deliverance, preservation, release, and safety. The word appears forty-five times and is the generic term for all that is included in God's salvation: forgiveness, deliverance, healing, well-being, safety, liberation and restoration. *Soteria* is wholistic and involves the total human being—physical, emotional, relational, social, and spiritual.

GOOD NEWS TO THE POOR
(Luke 4:18, 19)

After His baptism and temptation, Jesus "returned in the power of the Spirit to Galilee" and began His public ministry by teaching in the Jewish synagogues (Luke 4:14, 15). His itinerary eventually brought Him to His hometown of Nazareth. There He was invited to read the Scripture and make appropriate comment in the synagogue. He did so, reading from Isaiah 61. But His audience was unprepared for His next comment: "Today this Scripture is fulfilled in your hearing!" (Luke 4:21). Look at the quotation in Luke 4:18, 19 and seek to answer these questions:

Jesus was anointed by the Spirit of the Lord to preach the gospel to "the poor" (Luke 4:18a).

Who are "the poor"?

Why preach to these people?

This "gospel to the poor" would involve a number of ministries (Luke 4:18b, 19). Name each ministry and those for whom it is intended:

Look up Isaiah 61:1, 2. Where did Jesus stop His quotation? Why?

The importance of the stopping place Jesus' acknowledged in His reading is that thereby He differentiated the "kingdom ministry" for the present era, including unto our time, and that which will only follow His ultimate return. List the things Luke 4:18, 19 say are for *today.*

 BEHIND THE SCENES

Many have seen in the phrase "the acceptable year of the Lord" a reference to the "year of Jubilee" described in Leviticus 25. This year of liberation occurred every fifty years and was designed to "level" society by keeping the Jewish community balanced, lest some become extremely wealthy and powerful while others became extremely poor and powerless. Thus, each generation was to observe a "year of the Lord's favor" when fields lay fallow, persons returned to their family property, debts were cancelled and slaves set free. Beginning with the Day of Atonement, it was a year of "doing justice" and "loving mercy" (Mic. 6:8). Thus, it was a year of "jubilee" and joyful liberation. See "Jubilee" in *Nelson's Illustrated Bible Dictionary,* pages 600–601 (Thomas Nelson Publishers, 1980).

Jesus announced that the age of fulfillment had arrived. The hope of Israel for a messianic age had come, because Jesus, the Messiah, had come. He had come to proclaim the "good news" of true liberation for "the poor." But why the poor? Why does the God of Israel seem to have a special concern for the weak, oppressed, and impoverished? What does it say in Deuteronomy 24:17–22?

In the Gospel of Luke this special focus on the poor is particularly evident in Jesus' ministry to those who were economically disadvantaged, socially outcast, legally powerless, or morally bankrupt. They were the "sinners" He came to seek and to save. From these passages in Luke identify those to whom Jesus came to minister:

5:27–32

7:1–10

7:11–15

7:36–50

8:26–39

10:30–37

14:12–14

16:19–31

17:11–19

18:1–8

19:1–10

21:1–4

This focus should not surprise us in light of the fact the author of this gospel, although a well-educated doctor, was himself an "outsider." Luke was a Gentile. And so he included

Jesus' words in the synagogue at Nazareth about Elijah's feeding of the widow of Sidon and Elisha's healing of the Syrian Naaman. Like Luke himself, they were Gentile "outsiders"! No wonder the people in the synagogue were furious and drove Jesus out of town. This was not "good news"! These were not the people God should be concerned about . . . so they thought. "The gospel" is only for the "right people." But Jesus said such people *were* the right people!

Good news to "the poor" continued to be the focus of ministry after Jesus returned to heaven. The early church continued Jesus' ministry, and, like Him, found the greatest receptivity to the "good news" among common, ordinary, "poor" folk—both Jews and, especially, "outsiders" (Gentiles). Thus the apostle Paul wrote: "For you see your calling, brethren, that not many wise according to the flesh, not many mighty, not many noble, *are called*" (1 Cor. 1:26). Why was this so? Find your answers in these passages:

1 Cor. 1:27–31

James 2:5

SIGNS OF THE KINGDOM
(Matthew 11:1–5)

Yes, the Messiah had come. But where were the "signs of the kingdom"? What evidence was there God's kingdom had arrived? Were "the poor" having their world changed? Of course, multitudes were, as they received Jesus' ministry, but still:

• The pagan Roman rulers continued to dominate the life of the Jews.
• Religious hypocrisy seemed unchecked. Jewish religious leaders continued to burden the people with their legalism.

Where was God's promised judgment upon the wicked? Why was there so little justice, so little righteousness? Even the powerful preacher of righteousness, John the Baptist, was thrown into prison by Herod Antipas. Had not Zacharias, his father, prophesied that the Lord God of Israel would save His people from their enemies and from the hand of "all who hate us"? (Luke 1:71)

John himself had second thoughts about the messianic ministry of Jesus and sent two of his followers to ask Him a question. What was the question? (Matt. 11:3)

What was the answer Jesus sent back to John? (Matt. 11:4, 5)

What can we learn about God's passionate priorities with people from this answer?

Jesus' answer to John is a reference to Isaiah 35:5, 6, which described the coming glory of Zion when God's righteous rule would be vindicated. The desert would "blossom as the rose," "the glory of the LORD" would be seen, and a "Highway of Holiness" would be established (Is. 35:1, 2, 8). "Good news" indeed! What was Jesus saying by alluding to this passage? Good news *is* being preached to the poor! Signs of the kingdom *are* taking place! Yet Jesus recognized that many sincere people were confused and stumbled because His ministry and teaching did not fit politically preconceived ideas of the Messiah. Thus He concludes His message to John with special words. What are they? (Matt. 11:6)

THE "SIGN OF JONAH" (Matthew 12:38–45)

Especially offended with Jesus were the Pharisees. Their increasing opposition caused Him to become increasingly careful and strategic in His ministry. He did not stop forgiving, healing, delivering, and releasing the people. In fact, "great multitudes followed Him, and He healed them all" (Matt. 12:15). Not even the Pharisees' evil threats could overcome Jesus' compassion for people in need. But He warned them not to "make Him known, that it might be fulfilled which was spoken by Isaiah the prophet . . ." (Matt. 12:16, 17). Look up the passage in Matthew 12:18–21 which is a quotation of Isaiah 42:1–4. Note:

For what ministry was Jesus anointed with the Spirit? (v. 18a)

To whom was this ministry directed? (v. 18b)

How would this ministry be carried out? (vv. 19, 20a)

What would be the ultimate goal of this ministry? (vv. 20b, 21)

Strategic silence—"till He sends forth justice to victory"! In spite of such "signs of the kingdom," the Pharisees still demanded of Jesus: "Teacher, we want to see a sign from You." How could they be so blind? How could they be so calloused? Notice Jesus' very pointed response in Matthew 12:39–42:

What was "the sign" that would be given?

Why this "sign"?

What is the point of the contrast between the response to this "sign" in the Old Testament story and the response of the Pharisees?

"The sign" of greatest significance was the Resurrection. It was that which would "send forth justice to victory"! For those who persisted in unbelief, it would become a sign of eventual judgment. But for those who believed, it would become a sign of ultimate victory! What meaning does each passage hold as a promise to us by the "sign" of Jesus' resurrection?

John 14:19

1 Cor. 15:22

1 Cor. 15:54–57

Because He lives, we shall live also! "For as in Adam all die, even so in Christ shall all be made alive" (1 Cor. 15:22). "Then shall be brought to pass the saying that is written: 'Death is swallowed up in victory. O Death, where is your sting? O Hades, where is your victory?' The sting of death *is* sin, and the strength of sin *is* the law. But thanks *be* to God, who gives us the victory through our Lord Jesus Christ" (1 Cor. 15:54–57).

AUTHORITY IN THE KINGDOM
(Matthew 28:16–20)

Jesus operated with "kingdom authority." He *had* authority because He operated *under* authority. Even a Roman centurion recognized this (Luke 7:1–10). Write your perception of the parallel made in the centurion's wise deduction about Jesus' power.

Because Jesus came only to do the will of His Father, when He spoke the liberating rule of God was released. Things happened . . . godly things! People were set free, for He taught "as one having authority," not as the teachers of the Law (Mark 1:21, 22). In the following passages identify that from which people were set free when Jesus spoke with authority, the authority of His Father:

Mark 1:23–26

Mark 2:3–12

Mark 4:35–41

The *most amazing* fact about "kingdom authority" for kingdom ministry is how Jesus delegated authority to His disciples. He sent out the twelve disciples, giving them "power" *(exousia)*, saying, "Freely you have received, freely give" (Matt. 10:1, 8). Look at verses 7 and 8 and list the five things the disciples were given authority to do:

1.

2.

3.

4.

5.

Likewise seventy others were sent out and also received "powerful authority." Upon their return they were joyfully exuberant that "even the demons are subject to us in Your name" (Luke 10:17). Please note Jesus' response to their enthusiasm in Luke 10:17–20:

What did Jesus see when they cast out demons? (v. 18)

Why did this happen? (v. 19)

What was even more significant than such "powerful authority"? (v. 20)

These two episodes relate to the sending out of Jesus' disciples only to "the lost sheep of the house of Israel," which has been called His "local commission" (Matt. 10:5, 6). It is His first introduction of disciples to the awesome privilege of kingdom ministry in kingdom power. Next, He will give His global "Great Commission" to His church for all time, to *go* and "make disciples of *all* nations" (Matt. 28:19, 20). Turn to this passage in the last chapter of Matthew and explain the basis on which Jesus gave this worldwide commission. Note the "therefore" in verse 19 pointing back to verses 16–18.

The resurrected Christ had been given all-encompassing *exousia* (authority) "in heaven and in earth." His decisive victory over the kingdom of darkness was the basis of His commission to the nations. He had broken, once and for all, the power of death and hell. The world must know!

The Book of Acts records what happened when His disciples went in His authority and in His name preached good news, declared forgiveness of sin, healed the sick, cast out demons, and raised the dead. What do these passages promise or say as a sample of what *would* happen or what *did* happen when kingdom people moved with kingdom authority into kingdom ministry?

John 14:12

John 14:14

Acts 4:13

Acts 17:6

 FAITH ALIVE

"Greater works" than Jesus Himself is an astounding promise. No, not "better works," but "greater" works . . . on a *greater scale:* more healings, more exorcisms, more resurrections, because His witnesses have multiplied His ministry thousands of times over as they extended His kingdom rule from Jerusalem to the ends of the earth. And there is no "expiration date" on these "greater works"!

The rapid and widespread growth of the Pentecostal and Charismatic movement in the twentieth century is living proof "greater works" are for today wherever people simply believe and ask. And more people are believing and asking than ever before! Lord, we believe; help our unbelief!

Like the earliest disciples, we, too, filled with His Spirit, are called to be His witnesses—doing the works of Jesus. The conditions are believing and asking in His name. We have been given resurrection-based authority to act on His behalf. Let's believe it. Let's ask in His name—-for *His* glory! If not now, when? If not us, who?

KEYS OF THE KINGDOM
(Matthew 16:18, 19)

The "keys" of understanding and authority were being *kept* from God's people, and Jesus didn't like it. He pronounced judgment against the scribes and Pharisees, calling them "hypocrites." They "shut up the kingdom of heaven against men . . . neither going in themselves, nor allowing those who are entering to go in" (Matt. 23:13). They used the keys of supposed "Bible teaching" wrongfully. They sat in the "seat of Moses," teaching others to keep the very Law they broke. "They say, and do not do," charged Jesus. "For they bind heavy burdens, hard to bear, and lay *them* on men's shoulders; but they *themselves* will not move them with one of their fingers. But all their works they do to be seen by men" (Matt. 23:3–5).

In the Parable of the Wicked Vinedressers Jesus vividly described why judgment would fall on the scribes and Pharisees (Matt. 21:33–46). Again, let's ask those three key questions of this kingdom parable:

What is the point, and what kingdom truth is contained in it?

How does this kingdom truth differ from popular understandings?

How should true disciples with ears to hear respond to this truth?

BEHIND THE SCENES

Like the fig tree, the vine and vineyard represent the people of God. Isaiah 5:1–7 describes God's disappointment over His vineyard, Israel, which He carefully planted and cultivated. Instead of the expected good grapes, wild grapes resulted. The Owner had done everything He could. He pruned the vines, dug up the vineyard, but to no avail. What is He to do? "I will lay it waste," declares the Lord. With this background, the parable in Matthew 21 describes the wickedness of the vinedressers to whom the vineyard was leased. Not only did they neglect the garden and lose the harvest, but they killed the owner's servants (the prophets) and ultimately killed the owner's son, who was the heir, so they could seize his inheritance. How despicable! What will the owner do? He will "destroy those wicked men miserably, and lease *his* vineyard to other vinedressers who will render to him the fruits in their seasons" (Matt. 21:41). The destruction of the temple, the sacking of Jerusalem, and the disbanding of the Jewish nation in A.D. 70 was the fulfillment of this prophetic parable.

The kingdom of God was thus being taken away from those resisting Christ's promise, power, and authority; and He said the kingdom would be given to those "bearing the fruits of it" (Matt. 22:43). Isaiah prophetically predicted the leaders of God's people would be removed from their position, and the "key of the house of David" would be given to those who would responsibly "open, and no one shall shut; and . . . shut, and no one shall open" (Is. 22:22).

This background of "keys" in God's Word helps us to understand Jesus' words to Peter when he made his great confession of his faith in the messiahship of Jesus as God's Son. What did he say? (Matt. 16:16)

Peter represented the new "nation" who would receive the "keys of the kingdom." Turn to this important passage and let's see if we can answer these questions (Matt. 16:13–19):

Who builds the church, and whose church is it?

What will not be able to stand against this church?

To whom are the "keys of the kingdom" given and for what purpose?

Jesus said He would build *His* church. Not even "the gates of Hades" would stand against it. The best understanding of this phrase is "the gates of death or hell." It is a reference to His resurrection which, achieved through His Cross, is the foundation of the church. Thus, the apostle Paul declared, "No other foundation can anyone lay than that which is laid, which is Jesus Christ" (1 Cor. 3:11).

Kingdom ministry is Jesus' ministry, and He's transmitted it to us in His name and by His authority. He is the Messiah whose words and works fulfilled His Father's will to redeem a sinful and fallen world. He was anointed by the Spirit of God to proclaim the kingdom of God. And by this same Spirit He anoints us as His disciples to be His witnesses to the ends of the earth.

"Greater works" are now possible because He has returned to the Father and sent His Spirit. Kingdom ministry not only continues, it expands. But kingdom ministry requires kingdom power. In our next lesson, we will discuss the work of that power in us to overcome whatever the world, our flesh and the Devil may throw at us.

Lesson 8/Conflict and Victory of the Kingdom

In the coming of Jesus as Messiah, God's kingdom won a decisive victory over the kingdom of darkness. The crushing defeat of death and hell was a massive breaking of sin's power and sin's arch-proponent, Satan. This decisive victory then ensures an ultimate victory *someday!* But in the meantime, the intensity of the battle increases. Like a mortally wounded animal, our Adversary can be extremely dangerous and tirelessly seeks revenge. Knowing his time is short, he wages intense warfare against God's kingdom and its citizens.

Dead fish float downstream, but as those alive in Christ, we're going against the "current" of "this present evil age" (Gal. 1:4). Like Alaska King Salmon swimming upstream to multiply, the King's "fish" (that's our historic symbol!) must swim against the tide of the times. When we receive Jesus Christ as Lord and enter God's kingdom, we are transferred from a kingdom of death into a kingdom of life. We now are alive in Christ and destined for a different direction—one directly opposite "the flow" of this world. See 1 John 2:15–17 and list the essential traits of "the world."

We are Christ's, and we face new pressures, opposition, tribulation, and even persecution. Jesus Himself faced such an "adverse flow" and warned His followers they would face the same. But the result would also be the same, namely, great reward! What is promised in His words of encouragement? (Matt. 5:10–12)

Life in the kingdom includes conflict with another kingdom. In this lesson we will consider both the nature and source of this conflict as well as the binding of and protection from the one who opposes citizens of God's kingdom.

THE AGE-LONG STRUGGLE
(Revelation 12:1–17)

The conflict on earth between the kingdom of God and the kingdom of Satan is but a mirror of the conflict in the heavenly realms. Behind the struggle between good and evil in our world is the struggle between God and Satan in the unseen world. This great conflict has been waged since the beginning, even before God's right to rule over His creation was contested by the serpent in the Garden of Eden (Rev. 12:7). This conflict between God and Satan has continued throughout this age.

But with the coming of the Messiah, Jesus Christ, the conflict intensified greatly. Why? Read 1 John 3:8 and write your answer.

Now read Revelation 12:1–6, and let's seek to answer the following questions:

Who are the two key "players" ("signs") in this conflict? (vv. 1–3)

What did the dragon intend to do to the newborn child? (v. 4)

Why did the dragon intend to do this to the newborn child? (Note how this newborn baby boy is described in v. 5a.)

But what happened to the woman's child? (v. 5b)

What happened to the woman? (v. 6)

Does this story remind you of another story? Of course it does! It is the story of Jesus. From the time of His birth when King Herod attempted to kill Him (Matt. 2:13–18), Jesus was in constant danger as even religious leaders attempted to take His life (Mark 3:6). But when it came time for Jesus to die, it was by God's plan and by Jesus' own choice (John 10:18) that He died on a cross in Jerusalem as the Lamb of God to take away the sin of the world (John 1:29, 35). Thus, even in death, Satan had no power over Jesus. In fact, the Cross was an unparalleled defeat for Satan and his forces (Col. 2:15) and the Resurrection a decisive blow against the kingdom of darkness as death died and Jesus rose to live forevermore. Hallelujah! What a Savior! What a strategic and significant victory! Now, take the five references used in this paragraph, look them up, and write your own description of the "conflict unto victory."

Now let's go on with the story. Read Revelation 12:7–10. Again, let's attempt to answer some key questions.

Where did war break out, and who were the opponents? (v. 7)

Who won, and what happened to the dragon and his angels? (vv. 8, 9)

As a result of this great "victory," what has now "come"? (v. 10)

Indeed, Satan and his angels have been decisively defeated. The deceiver of "the whole world" and the "accuser of our brethren" has been cast down.

But heaven's great victory must yet be secured on earth. God's kingdom must yet come on "earth as *it is* in heaven." Let's read on. Look at Revelation 12:11–17. Write down what now takes place on earth.

How did the "brethren" (believers) overcome their "accuser"? (v. 11)

What did the Devil do when cast to earth? (vv. 12, 13)

What happened to the "woman" who gave birth to the male child? (vv. 14–16)

What did the frustrated dragon do then? (v. 17)

The message is clear: God won; Satan lost! He lost in his attempt to destroy the male child, Jesus Christ, the Messiah. Further, he was unable to kill the child's mother (most likely a reference to the true remnant of God's people). Now he attempts to kill the rest of "the woman's offspring" (believers in Jesus Christ) who "keep the commandments of God and have the testimony of Jesus Christ" (Rev. 12:17). *But these are the "overcomers" in verse 11!* Look at it, because it's you and me! And again Satan will lose! Throughout the years, there have been many martyrs for the cause of Christ and will still be others until He returns; but ultimately we all overcome the Dragon by the blood of the Lamb, the word of our testimony.

This is the nature of the age-long conflict between God's kingdom and Satan's kingdom. It is a life-and-death struggle. But in Christ the decisive victory has already been won and the guarantee of ultimate victory secured for God's kingdom and His people. And even though they may suffer and some may even die, the final outcome is certain!

 PROBING THE DEPTHS

At least three interpretations have been suggested to explain the expulsion of Satan from heaven. We propose they are *all* true and blend together—like a play with one plot, but three *acts* or key developments.

The *first* "casting down" may have occurred before the creation of the heavens and the earth. Isaiah 14:12 speaks of one called "Lucifer, son of the morning," who had "fallen from heaven" and was "cut down to the ground." Ezekiel 28:13–19 describes an "anointed cherub" who was "in Eden, the garden of God" and was "perfect in your ways from the day you were created, till iniquity was found in you." But then due to arrogant pride, this angelic being was "cast . . . to the ground." In both passages the descriptions are applied to contemporary wicked rulers apparently through whom Satan himself ruled. Some hold that their "casting down" is a reflection of Satan's own "casting down" before the beginning of Creation. As his emissaries their destiny is that of their master.

Second, in Christ's life, death, and resurrection Satan was "cast down." In Luke 10:18 Jesus told the seventy, upon their return from casting out demons in His name, He saw "Satan fall like lightning from heaven." Jesus Himself also clearly indicated the reason He cast out demons was because Satan, the "strong man," had been bound (Matt. 12:28, 29).

Third, ultimately Satan, along with the Beast and the False Prophet, is cast into the lake of fire, and their power to deceive is finally and fully destroyed (Rev. 20:10). If these interpretations are correct, the "casting down" of Satan shows his dethroning is that which was, is, and shall be, because God alone is sovereign over all He has made! Further help and insight may be found in such exegetical commentaries as *The Expositor's Greek Testament: the Synoptic Gospels* (Eerdmans, 1979 reprint) and the *New International Greek Testament Commentary on Luke* (Eerdmans, 1978).

THE "GOD OF THIS AGE"
(2 Corinthians 4:1–6; Ephesians 2:1–7)

Satan's defeat is progressively revealed in the Scriptures and progressively realized during redemptive history. Although decisively defeated and mortally wounded in the Cross and Resurrection of the Messiah, he is the age-long adversary of God's redemptive purposes until his ultimate destruction in the lake of fire. Until then, Satan continues as the "god of this age." Read 2 Corinthians 4:1–6.

What is Satan's primary strategy as the "god of this age"? (vv. 3, 4)

What is the answer to defeating this strategy of Satan? (vv. 2, 5, 6)

In a previous lesson we saw how conversion is viewed by the apostle Paul as being "delivered . . . from the power of darkness into the kingdom of the Son of His [God's] love" (Col. 1:13, 14). In Ephesians 2:1–7 the apostle vividly describes the dramatic contrast between life before and life after conversion to Christ.

"In Christ" a person has come under a new Lord. Such a person is liberated from the "god of this age" by the One who alone is the only true King and liberating Lord. His kingdom alone is based on the righteousness of God offered as a free gift to all who humbly repent and truly believe. All other gods are false and enslave their followers. Their kingdom is based on unrighteousness, for its ruler is Satan himself, the source of all evil.

BINDING THE "STRONG MAN"
(Matthew 12:22–32; Colossians 2:15)

The "binding" of Satan is the basic assumption behind exorcism and spiritual breakthrough! Why did Jesus say He cast out Satan's demons?

Matt. 12:28

Matt. 12:29

He first bound the strong man! In Christ's coming, Satan has been bound and God's kingdom has come. In the *heavenly realm* the victory is accomplished. How can we learn to apply this victory?

After His baptism, Jesus' authority over Satan is clearly seen in His consistent casting out of demons, beginning with an exorcism in the synagogue in Capernaum (Mark 1:21–28, 34). We have looked at Matthew 12:22–32 before. Let's look at it again, but this time let's seek to answer these three questions:

How did Jesus know the healing of blindness and dumbness required the casting out of demons in this case? (v. 22)

How did Jesus know the Pharisees thought He cast out demons by Beelzebub, the prince of demons? (v. 25)

What was the "unforgivable sin" of the Pharisees? (vv. 31, 32)

PROBING THE DEPTHS

Clearly these Pharisees committed the "unpardonable sin" when they accused Jesus of casting out demons by the power of Satan. They blasphemed against the Holy Spirit through whose power alone Jesus cast out demons. This is the original historical setting for the unforgivable sin of blasphemy against the Holy Spirit. Can such a sin be committed by someone today? Yes and no. Yes, for in a sense everyone who refuses to believe in Jesus Christ commits the "unpardonable sin" of unbelief. And unless they repent and believe in Him for their salvation they will ultimately be condemned (John 3:18–21; 16:9). No, in the sense of the Pharisees' sin of directly attributing the works of the incarnate Son of God to the Devil. This "unpardonable sin" could only be committed by those who saw Jesus in the flesh. But Jesus "broadens out" the principle of blasphemy against the Spirit to "whoever speaks against the Holy Spirit" (Matt. 12:32). However, it seems that such a sin is committed by persistent unbelievers, such as the Pharisees, not by true believers, such as disciples of Christ. Furthermore, although the writer of Hebrews (Heb. 6:4–6) warns of the possibility of an "apostasy" (literally "falling way") by a believer for which there is no repentance (and thus no forgiveness), he indicates that such an "unpardonable sin" is not at all probable. In fact, he writes he is "confident of better things concerning you [believers], yes, things that accompany salvation, though we speak in this manner" (Heb. 6:9). Thus, the committing of the "unpardonable sin" *by believers* is most unlikely. How could those who have been "enlightened, and have tasted the heavenly gift, and have become partakers of the Holy Spirit, and have tasted of the good word of God and the powers of the age to come" be so foolish (Heb. 6:4–6)? For the believer who is concerned about having committed such an "unpardonable sin," the very concern indicates the sin has not been committed! Those who have committed the "unpardonable sin" are unrepentant and thus are unpardonable.

It is clear that Jesus could see and operate in the invisible realm. This entire story is a clear illustration. The real battle was not against "flesh and blood" but against spiritual powers. Therefore, the casting out of demons required both the spiritual insight and power that only comes by the Holy Spirit. Such insight and power were evident in the life and ministry of Jesus after the Holy Spirit came upon Him at His baptism in the Jordan. In the words of the apostle Peter: "God anointed Jesus of Nazareth with the Holy Spirit and with power, [that He] went about doing good and healing all who were oppressed by the devil, for God was with Him" (Acts 10:38).

The key issue in casting out demons is the presence and power of the Holy Spirit. We need not bind the "strong man." He is *already* bound. We need not use special formulas. The name of Jesus *is* sufficient. What is needful is relationship with God through the presence and power of the Holy Spirit (see Acts 19:11 20). Then we can expect the works Jesus did, like exorcism, to take place, and even "greater works" because He returned to the Father and sent His Spirit.

TRIBULATION AND THE KINGDOM OF GOD
(Acts 14:21, 22; 1 Peter 5:6–11)

Tribulations and persecution are to be expected by those who follow Christ. As He was opposed and rejected, why should His followers expect to be treated any differently? "If the world hates you, you know that it hated Me before *it hated you*," said Jesus. "'A servant is not greater than his master.' If they persecuted Me they will also persecute you" (John 15:18–20). And because such opposition is normal, Jesus clearly warned His disciples about what would happen so they would not "be made to stumble" (John 16:1). The apostle Paul did likewise. How did he counsel new believers on his first missionary journey in Lystra, Iconium, and Derbe? See Acts 14:21, 22.

In fact, what did the apostle say in 2 Timothy 3:12 to all who "desire to live godly in Christ Jesus"?

But will not such teaching intimidate and discourage people from following Jesus? Yes, it could. But the apostle Paul, like Jesus Himself, felt the greater risk was not to tell people the cost of following Christ. Thus Paul continually told new converts that "no one should be shaken by these afflictions, for you yourselves know that we are appointed to this. For, in fact, we told you before when we were with you that we would suffer tribulation, just as it happened, and you know" (1 Thess. 3:3, 4). Faith is strengthened by knowing what to expect, for "to be forewarned is to be forearmed."

Furthermore, what have unbelievers to look forward to? Perhaps they may avoid persecution now by refusing to believe in Christ, but what does the future hold for such people? Read 2 Thessalonians 1:3–12, and consider the dramatic contrast between destiny of the believer and the unbeliever.

God did not "appoint us [believers] to wrath, but to obtain salvation through our Lord Jesus Christ" (1 Thess. 5:9). Therefore, believers do not fear "those who kill the body and after that have no more that they can do." Rather, they fear "Him who, after He has killed, has power to cast into hell" (Luke 12:4, 5). Because they fear God, they do not fear what men can do! Though they may suffer Satan-inspired opposition and persecution and even some may put to death, they know "not a hair of [their] head shall be lost," for they are protected from divine wrath and eternal death (Luke 21:16–19).

 WORD WEALTH

Tribulation and **wrath,** *thlipsis.* Used to describe the crushing of grapes or olives in a press. When applied to people it means pressure, oppression, tribulation, adversity and affliction. Its source, when directed at the righteous, is Satanic, human or both (1 Pet. 5:6–11). When directed at the unrighteous, its source is divine (2 Thess. 1:6, 7). In the latter case, the words used most frequently are "wrath," (*thumos*), signifying hot anger, passion, and boiling agitation; or "anger," (*orge*), referring to a more settled state or abiding habit of *thumos.*

SHEEP AMONG WOLVES
(Matthew 10:16–18)

Perhaps the most meaningful and significant picture of the contrast and relationship between the righteous and the unrighteous in this present age is that which Christ Himself used when sending His disciples out two by two. Let's turn to Matthew 10:16–18 and seek to understand the meaning and significance of the two contrasts found there.

In the first contrast disciples of Christ are characterized as sheep among wolves. In the second contrast they are characterized as both serpents and doves. The extreme danger of their situation requires a "wise innocence," such as Jesus Himself exhibited. It is essential they be sharp in discerning evil, yet innocent in doing evil.

Conflict is inevitable, because two dramatically different kingdoms are at war. The issues are eternally significant. Therefore, the citizens of God's kingdom may suffer tribulation and even death. But the outcome is certain because of Christ's victory over sin, death, and Satan. Thus, those who come under His authority and rule need have no fear. They shall ultimately stand as vindicated and victorious as their Master.

KINGDOM PROMISE:
THE KINGDOM BEGINS SMALL AND ENDS LARGE
(Matthew 13:31–33)

The parable of the Mustard Seed and the Leaven both describe dramatic contrasts. The mustard seed, proverbial for the smallest of seeds, is sown in a field by a man. But when it is grown it is one of the largest of plants, becoming a tree nearly ten feet tall in which even birds nest! Similarly, a small piece of leaven is "hidden" in about two pecks of meal by a woman baking bread. Yet this small piece of leaven leavens the entire lump of dough! So it is with the kingdom of God! Small beginnings do not necessarily mean small endings. Trials and tribulations ultimately bring victory.

Conflict and the kingdom of God are integrally related. Light has come into darkness, and the darkness seeks to quench it. Life has come into the realm of death, and death seeks to conquer it. In the Son of God was life, and the life was "the light of men. And the light shines in the darkness, and the darkness did not comprehend [overcome] it" (John 1:4, 5). Instead, the Light is overcoming the darkness, for the Life has conquered death. "For as in Adam all die, even so in Christ all shall be made alive . . . for He must reign till He has put all enemies under His feet. The last enemy *that* will be destroyed *is* death" (1 Cor. 15:22, 25, 26).

PART II
Kingdom Backgrounds

We have studied the foundational concepts that *introduce* the kingdom of God to our understanding and for our participation. Through our relationship to the King, we have obtained:

- citizenship in His heavenly kingdom (Phil. 3:20);
- a rich heritage by being made part of the lineage of faith (Heb. 11:40), and
- the sure promise of a bright and wonderful future (John 14:2, 3).

However, there are a number of more demanding underlying concepts related to the grand, glorious truth of the kingdom of God. In this section we will be looking at:

The Kingdom in the Book of Genesis (Lesson 9);

The Unfolding of Old Testament Perspectives on the Kingdom (Lessons 10, 11);

The Question of the Place of Israel and the Church in the Kingdom (Lesson 12); and

The Ultimate Climax of the Kingdom and the Present Possibilities (Lesson 13).

Let's gird up our minds and move into some strong truth, presenting and balancing the vital truth of the kingdom of God.

Lesson 9/The Kingdom in Genesis

"THE KINGDOM" AT THE BEGINNING

A study of the Bible's teaching about the kingdom of God and what it means to live in this kingdom is a way of allowing the Scripture's intended purpose to be fulfilled in our lives. It is a way of being made "wise for salvation" and "equipped for every good work." It is a way of allowing the Word of God to strengthen the foundation of our faith as we have been doing.

Having said this, it may come as a surprise to discover that outside the nearly one hundred times it occurs in the synoptic Gospels, the actual phrase "kingdom of God" is rather infrequent in the New Testament. And even though the concept abounds in the Old Testament, these exact words are nowhere to be found. However, as with the truth of the triune nature of God and the dual nature of Jesus Christ, the truth of "the kingdom of God" is far more prevalent in Scripture than the actual use of a specific phrase might suggest. It is proper, therefore, that we include in our study of life in the kingdom of God a look at the Old Testament, for it was these "Holy Scriptures" Paul had in mind when he wrote to Timothy. These scriptures are, of course, what formed the foundation of the faith all New Testament believers held in Paul's day, as the fulfillment of the Old Testament in Jesus Christ was first being realized.

GOD'S SOVEREIGNTY AND MAN'S RESPONSIBILITY
(Genesis 1 and 2)

"Who's in charge here?"

Why is this one of the first questions we ask when we are in a new situation? It's because we are designed for dependence.

We are sheep, not goats. We have a built-in desire to be led, to be given direction, to be given leadership. We are not made to be on our own, to be totally independent. Like a car, we are made for a driver.

The Bible begins with a description of God's creation of "the heavens and the earth." There are actually two accounts of Creation in the Bible: Genesis 1:1—2:3 and Genesis 2:4–25. Let's take a look at both of them.

When you read the first account of Creation in Genesis 1:1—2:3, what evidence do you find to indicate who's "in charge"? On whom is the focus? Who is the main character? An example is the phrase, "Then God said," which is repeated eight times in Genesis 1. Please write down what happens each time God speaks:

v. 3 *Let there be light; and there was light*

v. 6 *Let there be a firmament in the midst of the waters & let it divide waters from waters*

v. 9 *Let the waters under the heavens be gathered into one place & let the dry land appear*

v. 10

v. 14

v. 20

v. 24

v. 26

Clearly the focus is on God's sovereign, creative power, and the authority of His Word. His majestic might, His unique power, His creative wisdom—all come thundering through. There is none who even come close to His awesome greatness. God alone is Creator. He alone is the source of all that exists. And He alone sustains that which He has made. Therefore, every created thing owes its existence to Him.

Now note what is said over and over about what God created. What is the evaluation of God's creation? (vv. 12, 18, 21, 25, 31)

What does this phrase suggest about the One who's "in charge"? What kind of God is He?

And so with the psalmist David we exclaim: "The heavens declare the glory of God; and the firmament shows His handiwork!" (Ps. 19:1). God is indeed great, and all He has made is good—very good!

Now read the second account of creation in Genesis 2:4–25. It expands the story of the creation of humankind, the last and highest creation of God. The account begins where the first account left off: with man's creation in his Maker's own image.

 WORD WEALTH

Adam, *'adam.* "Man" or "mankind." It is translated about twenty times in the Old Testament as a proper name "Adam" and as a generic term for "man/mankind" over five hundred times. *'Adam* is possibly derived from the word *'adamah* meaning "soil" or "ground" from which man was formed (Gen. 2:7). *'Ish* and *'ishshah* are the words used to contrast the male and the female, respectively (Gen. 2:23).

Now go back and carefully read Genesis 1:26, 27. How is this "image/likeness of God" described in these verses? What is the point of similarity between God and humankind?

Does this surprise you? Is this point of similarity really unique? Are not animals likewise so created? Yes, they, too, were created male and female, and thus, like human beings, have procreative powers. But there is an important and significant difference, for the description of the creation of human beings as male and female is distinct and unique. Look again at Genesis 2:18, 21, 22. What is different and distinct in the way in which God made human beings male and female?

Now look again at verses 23–25. Because out of the male (*'ish*) came the female (*'ishshah*), they marry. In contrast to the animals, a monogamous relationship is the only proper way in which to express such unique unity. And this unity between male and female is described by the same word used to describe God's own unity, the word *'echad*.

> "Therefore a man shall leave father and mother and be joined to his wife, and they shall become one [*'echad*] flesh" (Gen. 2:24).
> "Hear, O Israel: The LORD our God, the LORD is one [*'echad*]!" (Deut. 6:4).

Amazing! Husband and wife are "one" (*'echad*) as God is "one." Thus, the "image" of God is expressed most fully in marriage, where two become one. God views marriage as a reflection of His very own nature.

FAITH ALIVE

If God views marriage as a reflection of His own essential unity, how do we view it? How should we view it? Why do some not view marriage this way today? What can we do to restore such a view of "holy matrimony"? If married, what can I do in my own marriage to make it a more adequate reflection of divine unity? What practical steps can I take to be "one" with my spouse? And if a marriage has ended in divorce, what could be done differently so that such "disunity" may not happen again? Do you know anyone needing to receive and experience God's forgiveness for divorce? Meditate on these thoughts and write your reflections. (If you are married, ask the Lord to fulfill Ephesians 5:21–33 in your marriage, noting the immediate context of Ephesians 5:15–20.)

Let's look again at this expanded account of the creation of humankind in Genesis 2:4–25. Notice the name for God now changes to a double name? What is it?

Why do you think this happens in this second account? What do you think is the meaning and importance of this change, especially in light of the focus on man and his relationship to the One who created him in His image?

WORD WEALTH

God, *'elohim.* The plural form of *'el* and is found over 2,500 times in the Old Testament, beginning in Genesis 1:1. *'Elohim* can be treated as singular, in which case it is used with singular verb forms and means the one supreme deity and is translated "God." *Yahweh* is the unique and sacred name for God revealed to Moses (Ex. 3:14) and is found over 5,000 times in the Old Testament. It is translated "the LORD" (note the capitals), in contrast to *'adonay,* which is translated "my Lord." *Yahweh,* in contrast to *'elohim,* is a proper noun, the name of a divine Person. The etymology of the word is uncertain, possibly coming from the Hebrew verb "to be." Thus, its meaning is better understood from the character of God as described by His words and works in the Old Testament. He is the "I AM" who was revealed to Moses as the eternal one, the God (*'elohim*) of Abraham, Isaac and Jacob who faithfully keeps covenant with His people as their Lord.

The Creation account clearly indicates God is the Creator of all. As the Source of all life, it is evident He alone is sovereign, "in charge." His creating and sustaining power make all things dependent on Him. If, as Creator, God is "in charge," what then is humankind's responsibility? List human duties of "delegated dominion" assigned in the following verses:

Gen. 1:28

Gen. 2:15

Gen. 2:19, 20

Why, of all God's creation, was humankind assigned these responsibilities? Were not the animals and birds also made from the ground as was man (see Gen. 2:7 and 19)? Why, then, should man be placed in charge of the rest of creation?

Take another look at Genesis 1:26, 27. What is the significance of the little word So at the beginning of verse 27?

In addition to these *ruling* responsibilities, was there any other responsibility man was given by his Creator? (See Gen. 2:16, 17.)

Why would God give man this moral responsibility, too?

MAN'S PROBATION AND PRESUMPTION
(Genesis 3:1–11)

Man's unique made-in-the-image-of-God nature gave him the "right" or the authority to rule over creation (Gen. 1:26–28). He was to "tend and keep" God's garden, the Garden of Eden (Gen. 2:15). He was allowed to eat freely of every tree of the garden, including the tree of life. But of the fruit of one tree, man was not to eat (Gen. 2:16, 17). Why do you think God made one tree "off limits"?

KINGDOM EXTRA

Genesis 2:8 says "the LORD God planted a garden eastward in Eden, and there He put the man whom He had formed." This verse suggests that Eden was larger than the garden, which may have been an enclosed area within "Eden." The location is identified as the headwaters of four rivers, only the last two of which are known today, namely the Tigris and the Euphrates Rivers (Gen. 2:14) in modern-day Iraq. Thus the story of the garden of Eden appears to be located in the well-watered valleys of ancient Mesopotamia.

What do you think is represented by "the tree of the knowledge of good and evil"? What was God prohibiting from man? (Note Gen. 3:6, 22.)

If people were not to know "good and evil" by firsthand experience, then how were they to know it? Why?

As God's responsible agent to tend, care, and rule over creation, man was put on probation by his Creator and Master, but blew it! Just one prohibition, and Adam and Eve could not pass the test of obedience. Rather than focusing on all they could enjoy, they were tempted by the serpent to focus on the one thing that was forbidden. Using doubt and deception, the Tempter asked, "Has God indeed said?" and claimed, "You will not surely die" (Gen. 3:1, 4). Thus, the man and woman succumbed to the serpent's cunning strategy and ate the "forbidden fruit." The underlying issue was trust. Would they believe and trust God and His Word, or would they believe and trust the Tempter's word? Tragically, they chose the latter. They sinned, disobeying God's command and violating His trust in them as His ruling agents over creation.

SIN'S WAGES AND GOD'S MERCY
(Genesis 3:12–24; 5:1—9:28)

The result of humankind's unbelief and disobedience was devastating! Innocence was lost. Nakedness became an embarrassment (cf. Gen. 2:25 and Gen. 3:7). Their relationship with their Creator became characterized by guilt rather than joy, and so they attempted to hide from Him (Gen. 3:8). When God called to them and asked, "Where are you?" the response of the man and woman was one of fear (Gen. 3:9, 10). And such fear resulted in defensive rationalizations for their disobedience when asked what they had done. What were their "answers"? Look at them and reflect on what they wrongfully imply about God their Creator.

The man's answer (Gen. 3:11, 12)

The woman's answer (Gen. 3:13)

God's answer is to spell out "the wages of [their] sin" (Rom. 6:23). Look at the judgments that were pronounced on the Tempter, the woman, and the man in Genesis 3:14–19.

What was the judgment upon the serpent?

What was the judgment upon the woman?

What was the judgment upon the man?

Notice that although only the serpent is directly "cursed" (3:14), that which was originally intended as blessings for the woman and man now become burdens, in a sense, a "curse." Childbearing will now be characterized by greatly increased sorrow and pain, and the husband will rule over the wife. Because the ground is "cursed" with thorns and thistles, man's working of the soil now becomes characterized by sweat and toil until the day he dies. But the most dramatic "wage" for their sin was to be driven out of the Garden of Eden (read Gen. 3:21–24).

Was God right? Did Adam and Eve "die" the day they ate of the forbidden fruit? List the immediate, eventual, and ultimate effects of "the Fall" as recorded in Genesis 3:

1. the immediate effects (vv. 7–13)

2. the eventual effects (vv. 14–20)

3. the ultimate effects (vv. 21–24)

The deadly "fallout of the Fall" is sadly evident in the subsequent chapters of Genesis. Adam and Eve's firstborn son, Cain, kills his younger brother Abel (Gen. 4). Adam himself dies, and the recurring phrase "and he died" in Genesis 5 underscores that the "wages of sin are death" (Rom. 6:23). By the time of Noah, the wickedness of humankind was so great "the LORD was sorry that He had made man on the earth, and He was grieved in His heart" (Gen. 6:5, 6). And so, through the Flood God visited judgment on humankind. Indeed, the "wages of sin are death" . . . in that all had sinned!

 FAITH ALIVE

Do you see anything in the fall of Adam and Eve that is characteristic of humankind today? Can you think of an experience when you "broke a rule"? What did you feel when you were confronted with your sin? What were the immediate effects of such sinning? And what were the eventual effects or results? And what of the ultimate effects? Is there not a sense in which all of us go through our own "Garden of Eden"? Do we not show our connection with our first parents in the way we so readily succumb to Satan's temptation, doubting and disobeying the rules? What can we learn from humankind's "original sin"? What could prevent such sin and its wages in our lives today?

Up to this point the picture is very dark. But in the midst of judgment is mercy! God's justice is only understood in the context of His love. He is a compassionate Creator. He is merciful in His might. His rules are only understood in light of His relationships, for He is a Creator who deeply desires fellowship with His creation made in His image. It was God who sought out the man and woman when they sinned (Gen. 3:10). See if you can discover the "light in the midst of the darkness."

Out of His unending love, what did God promise in Genesis 3:15?

Out of His undeserved mercy, what did God provide for Adam and Eve in Genesis 3:21?

Out of His amazing kindness, why did God drive Adam and Eve from the Garden? (Gen. 3:22–24)

Out of His great compassion, what did God promise after He spared Noah and his family in Genesis 8:20–22?

Hallelujah! Sin is not the end. It is but the beginning of God's rescue plan of redemption and restoration!

MAN'S PRIDE AND CONFUSION (Genesis 11:1–9)

After the Flood God mercifully multiplied the seed of Noah's three sons and through them eventually repopulated the earth. His command to them was, "Be fruitful and multiply, and fill the earth" (Gen. 9:1). But it took the Tower of Babel to accomplish this filling of the earth.

Read Genesis 11:1–9. What was the basic motivation for building the city and tower? (v. 4)

Why was God not pleased with this project? What was wrong? (vv. 5, 6)

Why the confusion of languages? (vv. 7–9)

Is God against unity? Is He against progress? What was the *real* problem with this "one language and one speech" generation? Perhaps we could call this the first instance of humanism, when man basically said by his actions, "I'll do it by myself . . . and take full credit for what I do!" It is clear humankind was motivated by pride ("make a name for ourselves") and used their unity wrongly. This is in dramatic contrast to Abraham, whom God promised to "make . . . great" (Gen. 12:2). Abraham clearly understood the source of his greatness. Thus, he refused to receive from the wicked king of Sodom any gift of supposed gratitude for returning his people to him lest the king should say, "I have made Abram rich" (14:21–24).

The primary revelation of God's sovereign rule is clear from the outset. The first chapters of Genesis indicate God is the Creator and Sustainer of all things. Therefore, all of His creation is under His authority. He is ruler of all. And to mankind, made in His image, God delegated authority over the earth. But man forfeited this authority, succumbing to the temptation of the serpent. He did not believe God's word and disobeyed, rebelling against his Creator's prohibition and eating of the forbidden fruit. As a result, creation came under a "curse" and man under a sentence of death. Mercifully expelled from the Garden of Eden lest he continue to eat of the Tree of Life and live forever alienated from his Maker, man now suffers the consequences of His disbelief and disobedience.

The wages of his sin brings death, both spiritual and physical. Now he is separated from God, and one day his spirit will be separated from his body, and he will die. And such death characterizes the entire human race. Thus the tragic result of the Fall is seen in the Flood, when all died except Noah and his family. Yet God had mercy and repopulated the earth through them. However, their descendants wrongfully used their unity to make a name for themselves, seeking their own honor rather than the honor of their Creator. So God confused their language, and seventy nations were the result. It is painfully evident humankind has rejected God's sovereign rule. Stubborn self-will rather than humble obedience characterizes mankind from the time of the Fall to the Tower of Babel. Although through Creation man knew of God's eternal power and divine nature, "they did not glorify *Him* as God, nor were thankful, but became futile in their thoughts, and their foolish hearts were darkened" (Rom. 1:21). It is against this dark backdrop God now makes a significant and strategic choice. This is the focus of our next lesson.

Lesson 10/Kingdom Heritage

Lesson 9 focused on the primary foundation for understanding God's kingdom found in the first eleven chapters of Genesis. Five major truths are evident:

1. God is in charge because He alone is the Creator and Sustainer of all creation.
2. God made all things "good," including man, whom He made in His own image and gave dominion over the earth.
3. Man succumbed to the serpent's temptation and thereby lost his right to rule on God's behalf.
4. The "wages of sin *is* death,"—both spiritual and physical. Man lost relationship and fellowship with God because he did not trust and obey his Creator. And so death characterized the race as humankind continued in unbelief and disobedience.
5. Most important, God had a "rescue plan." Sin was not the last word. Rather, it became the beginning point of God's redemptive love.

We now come to a major turning point in God's redemptive work for human salvation and restoration. Although God's mercy is evident in the earliest chapters of Genesis, it is not until we come to Abraham that we see clearly God's redemptive choice of a man through whom He will bless and rescue humankind from their unbelief, disobedience, and rebellion against their Creator.

GOD'S FOCUSED CHOICE AND FAR-RANGING COVENANT
(Genesis 12:1–3)

A "hinge point in history" occurs in Genesis 12. Although God's gracious choices are evident in the way in which He graciously worked through Seth and Noah and their descendants (Gen. 4—11), He now makes a "focused choice" to work primarily through one man and his descendants. God now makes a far-ranging covenant with an uncircumcised descendant of Shem. His name is Abram (later Abraham), a "Gentile" from the pagan, idol-worshiping city of Ur of the Chaldees.

WORD WEALTH

Covenant, *berit.* The word used to describe an "agreement" or a "contract" between individuals, nations, and between God and man. Although the etymology of *berit* is uncertain, the ancient suzerainty treaty found in the Near East is a key in understanding the form of God's covenant with His people (see M. G. Kline, *Treaty of the Great King,* Eerdmans, 1963). Like the agreement between a king and his subjects, God's agreement with Abraham and his descendants included His promised blessings and their required allegiance and obedience. Thus, the Septuagint (the Greek translation of the Hebrew Old Testament) translates God's *berit* with *diatheke,* a word used to describe a unilateral "agreement" between two unequal parties rather than *sunetheke,* a word which describes a bilateral agreement between equal parties. God, as sovereign Lord, initiates, defines, and establishes the content and conditions of the "contract." Its initiation is unconditional, based on God's sovereign love, but its fulfillment is conditional, based on man's continued allegiance and obedience.

God's intention is to bless Abram. Abram's part is to obey and leave town. He is to go to a land God will show him—the land of Canaan, hundreds of miles to the west. But why did God choose Abram? No reason is given. Again, God's gracious choice underscores His amazing and undeserved mercy and love. The question is not Why did God choose Abram? Rather, it is, Why did He choose anyone at all?! And the answer is, Because of His love!

Let's take a closer look at what God promised in His gracious covenant with Abram. Read Genesis 12:2, 3 and list "the blessings":

What an amazing list! But there is more, much more! Look again at verse 3. Were such blessings to be restricted only to Abram and his descendants? To whom else was blessing to come?

What does this tell us about God's choice in choosing to bless Abram? Was it an exclusive or an inclusive choice?

We could call this the "bottom line" of the covenant with Abram. And what a "bottom line" it is!

Now look again at the last part of verse 3. What does it tell us concerning God Himself? What is His intention or preference as it relates to blessing or cursing people through Abram? Which does He prefer—to bless or curse? Why?

But there is more! To and through whom else were such multiple and widespread blessings directly promised?

Gen. 26:2–5

Gen. 28:12–14

And there is still more! Read Genesis 17:7. In addition to the material blessings of prosperity and property, what else does God promise to Abram and his descendants?

We can call this the "top line" of God's blessing to Abram. And what is particularly significant is that this "top line blessing" is also for the "bottom line." Through Abram and his descendants "all the families of the earth" are likewise to be blessed. And so, his name is changed from Abram ("exalted father") to Abraham ("father of many"). Multiplication of Abraham's offspring and *through* them multiplication of his blessing to a world is the focus and point of the name change.

The God of Abraham, Isaac, and Jacob is the God who desires to bless all the families/nations of the earth with far more than material blessings. He desires to bless them with Himself. This He expresses in the form of His "everlasting covenant" beginning in Genesis 17.

In addition to promising to "be God" to Abraham and his descendants, God's covenant includes an amazing promise. This is clearly seen in God's reason for delivering Abraham's descendants, the nation of Israel, out of bondage in Egypt. Look at Exodus 29:45, 46, and list the two other dimensions of the "top line blessing":

Thus, God intends through Abraham and his offspring to restore that which was lost in the Fall. He promised to Abraham and his descendants:

a. "I will be God to you" (headship)

b. "You will be My people" (relationship)

c. "I will be with/dwell among you" (fellowship)

This is the true blessing of the "top line" of the covenant made with Abraham. The fullness of this blessing is that which shall ultimately characterize God's kingdom. It is powerfully described in Revelation 21 and 22 when "the tabernacle of God *is* with men, and He will dwell with them, and they shall be His people. God Himself will be with them *and be* their God" (Rev. 21:3). And this top line of full blessing includes the "bottom line," for the word translated "people" is literally "peoples" (*laoi,* the plural form of *laos*). What a great and glorious prospect!

 WORD WEALTH

Families, nations, *mishpachah.* Refers to an extended family or a "clan," which in some instances would be larger than a "household" (*bet*) but smaller than a "tribe" (*sebet*) as in the case with the story of the detection of Achan in Joshua 7:16–18 as the search moved from "tribe" to "clan" to "household." In other instances it can be as wide as a "nation" (*goyim*) as in Genesis 18:18, a parallel passage to Genesis 12:3 where "family" (*mishpachah*) is used.

KINGDOM OF PRIESTS
(Exodus 19:3–6)

The nation of Israel had twelve tribes, the offspring of the twelve sons of Jacob, grandson of Abraham (Gen. 35:22b–26). Since the two sons of Joseph, Manasseh and Ephraim, were each named as separate tribes, they take the place of their father (Josh. 14:3, 4). Thus there were, in fact, thirteen tribes. However, the descendants of Levi—the Levites—were not counted as one of the twelve tribes. They had a special calling. They were the priests and assistants to the priests in the worship of the nation of Israel. Read Exodus 32:25–29. Why were the Levites set apart from the other twelve tribes?

And so it was that Moses declared: "Consecrate yourselves today to the LORD, that He may bestow on you a blessing this day, for every man has opposed his son and his brother" (Ex. 32:29).

Subsequently the Levites became known as the "priestly tribe" (see Josh. 18:7). What were the functions of the priests according to these passages?

Ex. 29:42–46

Ex. 30:7–10

The priests were the Levites directly descended from Aaron, the first priest. The rest of the Levites cared for the tabernacle and served the priests. This priestly ministry by the Levites was carried out on behalf of the other twelve tribes. They were God's intermediaries for His people.

Read Exodus 19:3–6. This is the first time the words *kingdom* and *priests* are tied together. Who is to become this "kingdom of priests"?

Why a "nation of priests" when they had a "tribe of priests"? Could it be that what the tribe of Levi did for the nation of Israel, the entire nation of Israel was to do for the nations? What does it say about Israel's relationship to "the nations" in these passages?

2 Chr. 6:32, 33

Is. 2:2, 3

Is. 49:6

WORD WEALTH

Kingdom, *malkuth.* "Sovereign power," "kingship" or "reign." The word for "king" *(melek)* is a common word in the Old Testament (over 2,500 times) and appears in modified form in most Semitic languages. *Melek* also is translated as "lord," "ruler," "captain," "chief," "prince," and so on. The use of *malkuth* refers to a king's rule or dominion more frequently than to the territory or land over which he ruled.

But there is another phrase at which we need to look. They were to be a "kingdom of priests" *and* a "holy nation." They were to be like their God—"holy." If they were to represent the God of Israel before the nations, they must be distinct and different from those nations. They must "obey their God fully and keep His covenant" (Ex. 19:5). In order for God to be their God, God's people must worship Him, and Him alone. Note the first two commandments found in the Ten Commandments. Write them out.

first commandment (Ex. 20:3):

second commandment (Ex. 20:4):

Idolatry must never characterize this "holy nation"! They are divinely different. The true and living God is the center and focus of their life.

WORD WEALTH

Holy, *qodesh.* "Apartness," "sacredness." It is used to describe anything separated from ordinary to sacred use. Thus the Sabbath is "holy," dedicated to the Lord (Ex. 20:8). It is a day of "ceasing," when a person stops normal activities and devotes or consecrates the time to the Lord. Dedication, separation, consecration to sacred purposes is the fundamental idea of *qodesh*. When applied to God it indicates His separateness from, and exaltation above, His creation. He is wholly other, apart, distinct, different, and transcendent. Further, when applied to God *qodesh* most frequently refers to His moral excellence and ethical purity (Is. 6:3). "Holiness" is that distinctive attribute of attributes in which all other attributes of God find their source and significance. God is, indeed, "holy." He is wholly separate and totally pure. Thus His people are called to be holy as He is holy—consecrated and cleansed for His purposes.

Repeatedly the Lord had told Moses why He wanted the Egyptian Pharaoh to "let My people go." See Exodus 4:22, 23; 5:1, 3; 7:16; 8:1, 27; 9:1, 13. What was the primary reason?

Above all else God desired Israel's worship, for it was out of the witness of their worship that surrounding nations would come to know the only true and living God, the "Holy One of Israel." His people were to be His "witnesses" that there was no other God. Read Isaiah 43:9–13. What was the clear point of contrast between the God of Israel and foreign gods?

THE DAVIDIC KINGDOM
(1 Samuel 8; 2 Samuel 7:1–17)

God Himself was to be Israel's King. But they proved to be disloyal subjects, a wayward nation. Too often their service was given to other gods who were no gods at all (Deut. 7:16; 2 Kin. 10:18, 19). Eventually the intended theocracy became a monarchy when God's people demanded "a king to judge us like all the nations" (1 Sam. 8:5).

Read carefully 1 Samuel 8:7, 8 and summarize how God interpreted their demand and why.

Years earlier, during the time of Moses, God had anticipated such a day would come. Read Deuteronomy 17:14–20.
If Israel wanted a king, what were to be the requirements for
such a king?

With strong warnings, God consented to the people's
demands and gave them King Saul through whom God would
rule His people. But he did not carry out God's commands.
Saul, who had begun so humbly, disqualified himself as king.
So God removed His anointing to rule from Saul and chose
and anointed as king a shepherd boy, David, "a man after His
own heart" (1 Sam. 13:13, 14). What does this phrase mean?
In what way was David different from Saul? Did he not sin
also? Compare 1 Samuel 15:17–26 with 2 Samuel 12:1–13
(see also Ps. 51) and summarize the fundamental difference.

Through King David and his descendants, God established a lasting kingdom (2 Sam. 7). To David's son Solomon,
who built God's house, God promised: "I will be His Father,
and he shall be My son." And, in contrast to Saul, He further
promised: "My mercy shall not depart from him" (2 Sam.
7:14, 15).

THE TALE OF TWO KINGDOMS
(2 Kings 17:7–20)

Sadly, King Solomon not only multiplied horses, he
multiplied wives! And they turned his heart from the true
God. To secure his kingdom, he married women from royal
families from the surrounding nations, "and his wives turned
his heart after other gods" (1 Kin. 11:1–4). Thus, in contrast
to his father David, Solomon's heart was divided and he was

"not loyal to the LORD his God" (1 Kin. 11:4). Read 1 Kings 11:9–13. What did the Lord say would happen because of Solomon's unfaithfulness?

To secure his rule King Jeroboam instituted the worship of golden calves to keep the people from going to Jerusalem to worship lest they come under rule of Solomon's son, King Rehoboam.

The tale of these two kingdoms—Israel in the north and Judah in the south—was largely one of persistent and pervasive idolatry. Of the nineteen kings in the north, not one was considered a "good" king. Meanwhile in the south, only eight of twenty were identified as "good." And on what basis did the writer of the Books of 1 and 2 Kings evaluate each king? See 2 Kings 17:19–23.

 BEHIND THE SCENES

The Egyptians portrayed many of their gods with animal images, including a "golden calf," which the Israelites made and worshiped when Moses was on Mount Sinai receiving the Ten Commandments (Ex. 32). Prior to the Exodus, the ten plagues in Egypt were intended as a judgment on the gods of Egypt (Ex. 12:12). They dramatically revealed the superior power and holy character of the God of Israel over the so-called gods of Egypt, the world's greatest nation at the time. Thus, the plagues were designed to show the God of Israel's transcendent power, so that, as God commanded, My name may be declared in all the earth" (Ex. 9:16).

When Israel conquered the Promised Land, they were to utterly destroy the inhabitants of the land lest they be tempted to follow their gods. Thus, just before his death, Joshua called Israel to wholehearted faithfulness to the God of Israel. He challenged them to "put away the gods which your father served on the other side of the [Euphrates] River and in Egypt . . . [including] the gods of the Amorites, in whose land you dwell" (Josh. 24:14, 15). "As for me and my house, we will serve the LORD" declared Joshua, and the people joined him in this covenant. But it only lasted until the next generation (Judg. 2:7–13). Seven times during the period of the judges Israel went through the cycle of idolatry, oppression, repentance and renewal. The gods of the pagan nations around Israel were a constant threat to their worship of the God of Israel. The pervasiveness of the idolatry of Israel's neighbors is dramatically and thoroughly described in an article titled "Pagan Gods" in *Nelson's Illustrated Bible Dictionary,* pages 429–436 (Thomas Nelson Publishers, 1986).

THE COMING KING AND KINGDOM
(Daniel 2 and 7)

In spite of the repeated warnings of the prophets, both Israel and Judah persisted in their idolatrous ways. They "stiffened their necks, like the necks of their fathers, who did not believe in the LORD their God. And they rejected His statutes and His covenant. . . . They followed idols, and became idolaters . . . until He had cast them from His sight" (2 Kin. 17:14, 15, 20). Ironically, the Lord used these very pagan nations as instruments of His righteous judgment, allowing the Assyrians to defeat, deport, and disperse Israel and the Babylonians to defeat and deport Judah.

Instead of being holy like the God of Israel was holy, God's people became worthless like the worthless pagan gods they served. Instead of their worship and service being a light to the nations and a witness to the true and living God, their worship and service was polluted and their witness deceptive. The "missionaries" were "converted" to the worship of the gods of the nations rather than converting the nations to the true worship of the God of Israel.

But in the midst of such tragic darkness, a ray of hope began to emerge. At the height of the Babylonian Empire, Daniel, a man greatly loved of God, was given a revelation of God's eternal redemptive purposes for His people. Through the dream and interpretation of the dream of a pagan king, King Nebuchadnezzar, Daniel understood that "the God of heaven will set up a kingdom which shall never be destroyed;

. . . it shall break in pieces and consume all kingdoms and it shall stand forever" (Dan. 2:44).

Compare the four parts of the "great image" in Daniel 2 with the "four great beasts" in Daniel 7. What do the descriptions suggest as to the nature and strength of these kingdoms?

Head of gold—first beast like a lion with eagle's wings

Chest and arms of silver—second beast like a bear with ribs in its mouth

Belly and thighs of bronze—third beast like a leopard with four wings

Feet of iron and clay—fourth beast, strong and terrible with iron teeth

Describe any kind of progression you see in the descriptions of these kingdoms:

During the fourth kingdom God's eternal kingdom appears. In Daniel 2 it is represented by the rock that struck the statue and became a huge mountain that filled the whole earth. In Daniel 7 it is "*One* like the Son of Man" to whom "was given dominion and glory and a kingdom, that all peoples, nations and languages should serve Him . . . an everlasting dominion which shall not pass away" (Dan. 7:13, 14). One of the rulers within the last kingdom prevailed "against [the saints] until the Ancient of Days [God] came, and a judgment was made *in favor* of the saints of the Most High, and the time came for the saints to possess the kingdom" (7:21, 22). A day is coming when God's kingdom will prevail, and all rival kingdoms will be destroyed. Hallelujah!

Lesson 11/Expecting the King's Arrival

The story of the beginnings of the human race and, accordingly, the Jewish race in Lessons 9 and 10 forms the necessary foundation for a proper understanding of the kingdom of God. This lesson will focus on the period of history from the time of the Jews' return from Babylon to John the Baptist. This 450-year period provides the immediate background to the New Testament. It is the backdrop against which Jesus' proclamation and explanation of the kingdom can be rightly understood and properly appreciated.

"Who's in charge?" was the seemingly unanswerable question that dominated the minds of the people of God during this perplexing period. "Where is the God of Israel? Why is there no king in Jerusalem? Why is there no word from God? Why does God not 'show up' and deliver His people? Have they not been cleansed from their idolatry? Then why does God not vindicate them and free them from rule of idolatrous nations? Why, why, why?" Every kingdom except God's kingdom seemed to be in charge! surely it was a time of disappointment and despair. Yet it was also a time of anticipation and hope. It was a time of significant and necessary preparation for the promised revelation of God's king and kingdom. So let's get started with this extremely important "chapter" of "His story," for it is the stage upon which the next scene of God's redemptive work will be revealed in a rather surprising and unexpected manner.

RETURN AND RESTORATION
(Ezra 1; Isaiah 45)

In 722 B.C. the northern tribes of Israel were defeated by the Assyrians and deported. In order to quell any uprising, the

Assyrians not only deported conquered nations, they dispersed them within the Assyrian Empire. Thus, national identity was weakened, if not destroyed, and troublesome enemies subdued. And so it was with Israel. They were deported and dispersed, losing their identity as a nation. And the same fate would have awaited Judah in the south if the Lord had not intervened at the last moment.

The dramatic deliverance of the southern kingdom from the Assyrian army in 701 B.C. is told in Isaiah 36 and 37; 2 Kings 18:17—19:37 and 2 Chronicles 32:1–23. In response to King Hezekiah's humility and prayer, the angel of the Lord killed 185,000 Assyrian troops surrounding Jerusalem, causing King Sennacherib to withdraw and return to Nineveh. And there, within a short time, two of his sons "struck him down with the sword." And so Judah was spared the fate of the northern tribes of Israel.

But Judah's judgment was only delayed, not removed. Increasing idolatry brought about her eventual judgment. However, in the sovereign wisdom of God, Judah's instrument of judgment was the Babylonian Empire rather than the Assyrian Empire, since the Assyrians had been conquered by the Babylonians in 612 B.C. Thus, in 586 B.C. when Judah was finally defeated and deported by the Babylonians, she was not dispersed as Israel had been by the Assyrians. And so the Lord preserved a remnant of His people through whom His saving purposes could continue.

Through three prophets God had anticipated Judah's deliverance from captivity in Babylon. It was the prophet Isaiah who predicted the actual return of God's people to the Promised Land. This prophetic word, given over 150 years before its fulfillment, can be found in Isaiah 45. Look at verses 11–13. Who would God raise up as His instrument of deliverance, and what would he do for God's people?

Through the prophet Jeremiah God had indicated that Judah's captivity would last seventy years (Jer. 25:12; 29:10–14). Why seventy years? Read 2 Chronicles 36:20, 21.

Through the prophet Daniel the Lord brought about the repentance necessary to release Judah back into the Promised Land. This repentance was occasioned by the reading of Jeremiah's prophetic word concerning the seventy years (see Dan. 9:1–3). Read Daniel's prayer in Daniel 9:4–19 and note:

what Daniel said about God Himself:

what Daniel said about himself and God's people:

what Daniel requested of the Lord on behalf of God's people:

Why do you think it was necessary for Daniel to partner in prayer with God's promise to restore Judah to the Promised Land? What does this suggest as to the place of man's participation in the fulfillment of God's prophetic word?

 FAITH ALIVE

What God promises will surely come to pass, but the "when" may sometimes depend on human response and obedience. God promised to give His people the land of Canaan as their possession, but the fulfillment of this promise was delayed a generation through unbelief and disobedience. God wanted to give the Ninevites opportunity to repent and avoid destruction, but Jonah delayed this from happening by running away. But oh, the mercy of God! He gave a second chance both to the Israelites and to Jonah! Opportunity can knock more than once in God's kingdom!

Are there any unfulfilled promises in your life? Is it due to fear, unbelief, or disobedience? As the Lord promised to the exiles in Babylon, "When you search for Me with all your heart . . . I will be found by you," so He will do for you. The promise still holds true. Partner with the promise in humble, sincere prayer like Daniel, and watch what the Lord will do. He *will* fulfill His word to you.

Daniel prayed; God answered! God not only fulfilled His promise through the prophet Jeremiah. He also fulfilled His word through the prophet Isaiah as He sovereignly moved upon the heart of the ruler of the Medo-Persian Empire. Read the proclamation of King Cyrus in Ezra 1:2–4. He released the Jews to return to Israel, but what else did he do?

Amazing! Surely "the king's heart *is* in the hand of the LORD, *like* the rivers of water; He turns it wherever He wishes" (Prov. 21:1), especially when His people humbly pray! God is, indeed, the King over all kings!

And so it was a second great "exodus" occurred as God delivered His people from captivity in Babylon just as He had delivered them from captivity in Egypt centuries earlier. Led by Zerubbabel, about 50,000 exiles returned and began rebuilding the temple. Although initially discouraged and delayed by opposition from the people in the land, they eventually completed the temple with great rejoicing in 516 B.C. They were greatly helped and encouraged in the building by the ministries of the prophets Haggai and Zechariah (Ezra 6:13–22). Proper worship of the God of Israel was again reinstituted and the Law of Moses carefully observed lest the tragic sins of the past with their devastating consequences be repeated.

BEHIND THE SCENES

As we have seen, three great empires profoundly impacted the history of Israel and Judah between 850 B.C. and 430 B.C. The Assyrians, who conquered Israel, were the dominant political power from approximately 850 B.C. to 612 B.C. The Assyrian king was seen as a regent on earth for the national god Asshur. Thus, Assyrian military campaigns were viewed, in part, as a holy war against those who failed to acknowledge Asshur's sovereignty. In 612 B.C. the Babylonians overthrew the Assyrians and became the dominant nation until 539 B.C. Babylonian King Nebuchadnezzar ruled during much of this period and brought the Babylonian Empire to its greatest point of influence as it conquered nation after nation, including Judah. In 539 B.C. the Medo-Persians overthrew the Babylonian Empire and released many peoples the Babylonians had conquered, including the Jews. Thus began a 200-year dominance by what was to become the most extensive empire the world had ever seen. The Medo-Persian Empire stretched from India to Africa.

EXPECTATION OF THE "DAY OF THE LORD"
(Malachi 3:1–5; 4:1–6)

Purified from their idolatrous ways, the exiles who returned to Judah conscientiously sought to please the Lord. Led by Ezra and Nehemiah, the people took on numerous reforms. Look at the following passages and briefly describe what "wrongs were righted":

Ezra 10:9–14

Neh. 5:1–12

Neh. 13:1–9

Neh. 13:10–14

Neh. 13:15–22

Neh. 13:23–27

Neh. 13:28–31

In light of such reforms, note the repeated theme found on the lips of Nehemiah in chapter 13 (vv. 14, 22, 29 and 31). This prayer reflects what the entire nation believed. They believed that as they faithfully sought to correct violations of the Law, God would "remember them" with favor. But as the years rolled, the people began to wonder, "Where *is* the God of justice?" They even went so far as to claim, "Everyone who does evil *is* good in the sight of the LORD, and He delights in them" (Mal. 2:17).

But God answered the questionings of the people through the prophet Malachi. Read Malachi 3:1. What did God say He would do? How would He answer? Who were the two people God would send to make things right?

1.

2.

What would the second messenger do when he came? (Mal. 3:2–5)

Why would he do this? (vv. 3b, 4)

Now look at Malachi 4:1–6, the final chapter in the Old Testament. Before "the day of the LORD," when God's

Messenger of the covenant comes, whom would God send to "prepare the way" for Him? And what would this forerunner do to "prepare the way"? (v. 6)

What does this mean, and why do you think this particular issue was the focus of preparation?

FOUR HUNDRED "SILENT YEARS"
(Amos 8:11, 12)

God's servants, the prophets, had been speaking on God's behalf for over four hundred years. Beginning with the "oral prophets" such as Samuel, Nathan, Elijah, and Elisha (who left no written prophecies) through the "writing prophets," such as Isaiah, Jeremiah, Ezekiel, and Daniel, the God of Israel had been calling His people to faithfulness to His covenant. And because the God of Israel was "King of all kings," He addressed also surrounding Gentile nations as well through prophets such as Jonah, Nahum, and Obadiah. In contrast to the "gods" of the nations, the God of the Bible was not dumb. He had been speaking though His prophets to the nations, and He expected response.

But then God stopped speaking through prophets. Read Amos 8:11, 12. Why do you think God did this?

And so it was, over three hundred years after this prediction by Amos, the prophetic word ceased with Malachi around 430 B.C. Thus begins what is known as the "four hundred silent years." From Malachi to John the Baptist there was no living word from the Lord to His people. Prophetic inspiration ceased. The God of Israel was silent.

As Amos predicted, God's people wandered "to and fro, seeking the word of the LORD" (Amos 8:12). In an attempt to meet this desperate desire to hear a word from God, the so-called "apocalyptic writers" (from the Greek *apocalypsis*, meaning "revelation") offered their interpretation of God's silence. In order to give an appearance of authority to their words, these men wrote using the names of well-known Old Testament individuals, such as Enoch, the Twelve Patriarchs, Moses, Ezra, Isaiah and Baruch. Their words were supposedly based on "revelations" that explained why evil seemed to triumph and how God's kingdom would intervene shortly to vindicate the righteous. Yes, God might no longer directly be speaking and actively working in history, said the apocalyptists, but that would all change in the near future. They claimed God's righteous kingdom would come from above and put an end to all evil earthly kingdoms. The wicked nations would be judged and God's righteous nation rewarded.

The prophetic hope of the Old Testament was slowly transformed from one of largely historical and earthly dimensions to one of primarily apocalyptic and heavenly dimensions. The increasing evil of the intertestamental period seemed to rule out the establishment of God's kingdom through merely an historical and earthly king. Only the divine intervention of God Himself from above could bring His kingdom to earth. Only the coming of God's own righteous kingdom could put an end to evil human kingdoms.

 KINGDOM EXTRA

Even within the Old Testament there is evidence of a growing transformation of the hope of the coming kingdom of God. An alternative to the popular hope of a human deliverer after the line of David is found in Daniel's visions of human kingdoms replaced by God's eternal kingdom (Dan. 2 and 7). This divine kingdom is brought by *"One* like the Son of Man" who comes from heaven (Dan. 7:13, 14). Such visions were the seed for the apocalyptic hope of God's inbreaking into human history from above.

Helpful insights into this significant transformation can be found in George E. Ladd's *A New Testament Theology,* pages 68–69 (Eerdmans, 1974).

Most important, God's chosen people considered themselves righteous, for they were now keeping the Law of Moses. Since only the Jews in Israel were close enough to travel to the temple in Jerusalem for worship, the study of the Law became the major focus in the synagogues dispersed throughout the Mediterranean world. In fact, in order to make sure no transgression of God's law occurred, Jewish religious leaders built "a fence around the Law." Oral laws interpreted how to properly keep the written laws found in the books of Moses. And it was the Pharisees who were the most conscientious in attempting to keep all the laws, both written and oral. The result of such a growing emphasis on the Law among the Jews was a stifling legalism that made keeping the Law, rather than God's gracious covenant, the basis of relationship with God. Keeping "the rules" became more important than loving God and people.

JOHN THE BAPTIST, A "VOICE"
(Matthew 3:1–6)

The kingdoms of the Medo-Persians, the Greeks and the Romans dominated the life of God's people, Israel. Would God's kingdom ever come? Would God ever speak again? Then it happened. After "four hundred silent years" the "famine" of a hearing of the word of the Lord was broken. And it happened through a most unusual man—John the Baptist. In fulfillment of Isaiah's prophecy, he was "a voice" crying in the wilderness (Is. 40:3–5).

In order to understand John and his message let's seek to answer three questions:

1. What was his message? (Matt. 3:2)

2. Who did he say he was? (Matt. 3:3, 4)

3. What did he? (Matt. 3:5, 6)

No wonder "Jerusalem, all Judea, and all the region around the Jordan went out to him" (Matt. 3:5)! They had not heard such a direct and clear word from God in over four hundred years! God was about to act. His kingdom was near. But John knew the people were not ready for such a significant event. Thus, as the "voice," he must prepare the people for the revelation of the "Word [made] flesh" (John 1:14, 15). As the "messenger" he must prepare the way for the coming of the "Messenger of the covenant" (Mal. 3:1). To use John's own words, "He must increase, but I *must* decrease" (John 3:30).

END OF AN ERA
(Matthew 11:1–15; Luke 3:1–14)

A "hinge point" in history occurred with John the Baptist. An era of divine silence and inactivity ended. God was speaking! God was acting! To appreciate the true significance of this amazing man, look at what Jesus Himself said about John the Baptist. Again, let's seek to answer three questions:

1. How did Jesus describe John? (Matt. 11:7–10)

2. What did Jesus say ended with John? (Matt. 11:13)

3. Who did Jesus say John really was? (Matt. 11:14; 17:10–13)

If John the Baptist is indeed "the Elijah who is to come," then the "day of the Lord" must be near (Mal. 4:5, 6). And if this is so, then proper preparation for this great "day" was essential. And what did John say was required of all who would so "prepare the way of the Lord"? Read Luke 3:3.

Further, what did John say should be the "fruit," or result, of such honest and humble repentance?

a. for the Jewish people? (Luke 3:7–11)

b. for tax collectors? (Luke 3:12, 13)

c. for the Roman soldiers? (Luke 3:14)

d. for families? (Luke 1:17; cf. Mal. 4:5, 6)

A profound rearrangement of priorities was required, said John. Right relationships and caring about people must take precedence over one's own interests. This was the kind of "fruit" of repentance that prepared the way for God to act.

The long, long drought finally ended! No longer did God's people have to endure the guesses of the apocalyptists. God Himself was again speaking. His kingdom was near. All flesh would see His salvation. Could it be the promised deliverance was about to take place? Could it be Zacharias, the father of John the Baptist, was right? He spoke with such assurance at his son's birth of the fulfillment of God's ancient oath to Abraham, that He would "grant us that we, being delivered from the hand of our enemies, might serve Him without fear in holiness and righteousness before Him all the days of our life" (Luke 1:74, 75)? Could this be the hour of God's great act of redemption? But why must we, who are already God's people, repent? Is not such repentance only for uncircumcised Gentiles, only for those who are outside the covenant? Is it not for the descendants of Abraham? Is it not a kingdom for the Jews, God's chosen people?

Lesson 12/The Church, Israel, and the Kingdom

God's kingdom is greater than any earthly expression of it. Man's great temptation is to make God's kingdom identical with the human manifestation of it. This was Israel's mistake. They attempted to make national Israel the limit of the focus and fullness of God's rule on earth. And the church has been tempted to do likewise. Such attitudes about God's kingdom tend to result in exclusive attitudes toward anything beyond the boundaries of the human institution. Thus, God is "boxed in," and His redemptive rule is confined to a given group. His activity is contained in familiar categories and external national, cultural and religious forms. Such an exclusiveness caused Israel to miss their expected Messiah. He just did not fit into their categories and forms. Likewise, the church can make the same mistake.

In order to avoid a "God-in-the-box" view of the kingdom, we will consider the relationship of the church to God's kingdom and to His ancient people, Israel. The proclamation of the kingdom is an announcement of good news about God's redemptive work in Christ, not the promotion of a human institution or society.

THE CHURCH AND THE KINGDOM
(Matthew 16:18–29)

Jesus intended to establish a "community of the king." Although He spoke infrequently about the church (only in Matt. 16 and 18), His emphasis on the kingdom implies an ongoing realm within which His will would be done and His rule honored. The passage that most clearly links the church and the kingdom is Matthew 16:18, 19. Again, we want to look at this important text in order to understand more clearly the relationship of the community of God's people to the rule of God's kingdom. Please turn to these verses and answer these questions:

Whose church is it?

Who builds this church?

What cannot stand against such a church?

Who is given the "keys of the kingdom"?

What is the connection between the building of the church and the use of the keys of the kingdom? (Acts 2:36–47)

The kingdom is the dynamic rule or reign of God. The church is the community of the kingdom, but the kingdom is never identified as the church. The kingdom is God's rule; the church is God's people. The church is the community of the kingdom, not the kingdom itself. The church and the kingdom are inseparably linked, but they are not the same. The action of the kingdom creates the church, but the church does not produce the kingdom. Without the kingdom there is no church, and without the church there is no kingdom. But the two remain distinct realities: the rule of God and the fellowship of men.

ISRAEL AND THE KINGDOM
(Acts 1:6, 7; Acts 19:8–10)

The close identification of the kingdom of God with the people of Israel is evident in the question the disciples asked Jesus in Acts 1:6: "Lord, will You at this time restore the kingdom to Israel?" The kingdom of God and the kingdom of Israel were synonymous in the minds of the Jews. Had not God chosen King David and his descendants through whom to rule His people and establish His kingdom forever? Israel and the kingdom of God were the same. To be an Israelite was to be in the kingdom.

Jesus' response in Acts 1:7 leaves the disciples' question unanswered. "It is not for you to know times or seasons which the Father has put in His own authority." Does this mean there will be a restoration of the kingdom to Israel? If so, what will be the nature of this restoration, even if we do not know the times or seasons of it? This is unclear at this point.

What was clear is that the disciples were to be witnesses to Jesus to the ends of the earth by the power of the Holy Spirit (Acts 1:8). And this witness was taken first to the Jews, even by the apostle to the Gentiles, the apostle Paul. It was Paul's custom to go to the synagogue first. Turn to Acts 19:8–10.

What did Paul boldly speak about in the synagogue in Ephesus for three months? (v. 8)

When unbelief forced Paul to leave and reason daily in the school of Tyrannus, what did Paul speak about there? (v. 10; cf. Acts 20:25)

And what was the result of Paul's ministry after two years? (v. 10)

Why did unbelieving Jewish people reject Paul's message of the kingdom? What was it that upset them? Was not the message of the kingdom for Israel? Yes it was! But not as popularly understood, namely, a kingdom exclusively for the Jewish people. Believing Jews, however, such as the apostle Paul, came to understand the true nature of the kingdom of God and its relationship to God's chosen people, the Jews. The message of the kingdom concerned the story of Jesus Christ as the fulfillment of the Jewish Scriptures. And this fulfillment was designed to liberate, not limit, the gospel, for Jesus came to be the Savior of the world (Luke 24:45–47). He came to save all who would believe, Jewish people and Gentiles alike.

PROCLAMATION OF THE KINGDOM
(Acts 8:12; Romans 1:16, 17)

The church plays a vital role in bearing witness to the kingdom. By the power of the Spirit "signs of the kingdom" accompanied the proclamation of the gospel of the kingdom in the Book of Acts. Healings, exorcisms, resurrections, and miracles demonstrated the presence of God's rule and confirmed the truth of God's Word. Like Jesus, the church proclaimed the kingdom in deed and word. Further, the church also had been given the keys of the kingdom with which to declare the basis of the forgiveness of sin both to those within and those not yet within the church (Matt. 16:18, 19; 18:15–20; John 20:21–23). Therefore, the witness to the kingdom was borne before "Gentiles, kings and the children of Israel" by men like the apostle Paul (Acts 9:15).

The nature of the kingdom Paul proclaimed was inclusive, not exclusive. Entrance was offered to all who believed, Jew and Gentile alike. Romans 1:16, 17 suggests the two reasons why Paul was "not ashamed of the gospel of Christ." What were they?

1.

2.

These two things make the gospel of Christ unique. There is no other gospel like it. It is not only powerful—able to save any who believe because it is a revelation of God's righteousness as a gift—it is universal. It is for Jews and Gentiles alike, for the gospel concerns the kingdom of God, not the kingdom of Israel. And the kingdom of God was far more inclusive than the nation of Israel. Why, it even had room for Samaritans (Acts 8:12)!

 BEHIND THE SCENES

A hidden message in the Book of Acts is the hesitancy of early Jewish believers to take the gospel to non-Jews. It took persecution to spread the word to Samaria, a threefold vision to get Peter to go to the house of Cornelius, the Roman centurion, and the dramatic conversion of Saul of Tarsus to take the gospel to the Gentiles. For the first seven to ten years "to the Jews first" looked more like "to the Jews only" as the Jewish church became preoccupied with the winning of their own countrymen both within Israel and beyond (Acts 11:19). It was the consistent rejection of the Jews that finally forced the gospel into more receptive Gentile territory (Acts 13:44–49; 18:4–8; 28:23–31). Jesus came as the Savior of the world, and that world included non-Jews. God's inclusion of non-Jews is dramatically underscored by the gift of the Holy Spirit poured out on "all flesh" without distinction—on Samaritans (Acts 8:14–17) and on Gentiles alike (Acts 10:44–47; 11:15–18). It is the outpouring of the Holy Spirit that transcends national, cultural, and ethnic barriers (Acts 1:8). A gospel prepared for a world is released to that world as Spirit-empowered witnesses obey the guidance of God's Spirit to take the gospel to those who have yet to hear the Good News about Jesus Christ (Acts 13:1–4; 16:6–10). For not only has the gospel been prepared for the world, the world has been prepared for the gospel by the sovereign working of the same Holy Spirit who causes people to hunger for the truth (Acts 8:26–39; 10:1–8). The great miracle of the Jewish church is that it became an international church by the power and persuasion of the Holy Spirit! For further study Donald McGavran's classic book *The Bridges of God: A Study in the Strategy of Mission* (Friendship Press, 1955) is most helpful and provocative in understanding how people come to Christ when the gospel is shared in a sensitive and contextualized manner without the trappings of foreign cultural forms.

ISRAEL AND THE CHURCH
(Romans 9—11; Ephesians 2:14–16; 4:4–6)

Several facts are clear from the Gospels.

First, Jesus did not intend to start a new movement either within or outside national Israel. His proclamation of the kingdom of God was intended to fulfill the Old Testament covenant and promises and bring Israel to its true destiny. He functioned fully as a Jew sent to the Jewish people. He understood His mission was to fulfill, not destroy, the Law (Matt. 5:17–48).

Second, Israel's leaders, and many others, rejected both Jesus and His message of the kingdom. His call to repentance and faith in the Good News met with resistance from the beginning (Mark 2:1–10). He was accused of blasphemy and eventually sentenced to die by crucifixion.

Third, a significant number did respond in repentance and faith. They continued in His word and became His disciples (John 8:31–34). Jesus called them the "little flock" (Luke 12:32). They were the "true Israel," the faithful remnant, who understood Jesus as the Good Shepherd through whom God would shepherd His people. These were the true "sons of the kingdom." They were the true people of God, the "Israel within Israel."

But what about Israel as a nation? Do they have a future? Will God's chosen people after the flesh have a part in the kingdom of God? Will the physical descendants of Abraham participate in the blessings of God's rule? Will God cancel His covenant and rescind His promises to His chosen people? In Romans 9—11 the apostle Paul wrestles with these perplexing questions. Please notice the main points of his argument about

Israel's future by answering the following questions from this section in the Book of Romans:

What are the special blessings God gave to the Israelites that still are in effect? (Rom. 9:4, 5)

Are all Israelites true Israelites? (Rom. 9:6–8)

What is the point of "the potter and the pot" analogy in Romans 9:18–24?

Why had Israel as a nation not "attained to righteousness"? (Rom. 9:30–32)

On what basis can Israel yet be saved? (Rom. 10:8–13)

What proof is there that God has not cast away His people, the Jews? (Rom. 11:1–5)

What is the "blessing" that has come as a result of Israel's rejection of the gospel? (Rom. 11:11)

What is the "mystery" Paul reveals concerning Israel's future, and when will it happen? (Rom. 11:25, 26)

Paul's conclusion is that God's mercy triumphs on behalf of both the Gentiles and the Jews, for He "committed them all to disobedience, that He might have mercy on them all" (Rom. 11:32). National Israel *does* have a future. They, too, with the Gentiles, will share in God's kingdom. Together they will be the people of God, the church. To make clear this truth, Paul uses the analogy of God's people as an olive tree (Rom. 11:16–24). If God could graft in the branches of a wild olive tree (the Gentiles), most certainly He can graft back in the natural branches which were broken off (the Jews)! God's ancient people, national Israel, will once again truly be the people of God!

God has but one people—His people. There is but one church—His church. The continuity of the people of God in the old and new covenant is seen in the mirroring of the twelve tribes in the twelve apostles. Although the New Testament maintains the distinction between "Jew" and "Gentile," just as it maintains the distinction between "male" and "female" and between "bond" and "free," in Christ such differences no longer make a difference, for all are saved by grace through faith in Him (Col. 3:10, 11). In Ephesians 2:14–16 Paul describes why such miraculous unity is possible. In your own words explain what Christ did and why He did it:

Thus, "in Christ Jesus neither circumcision nor uncircumcision avails anything, but a new creation. And as many as walk according to this rule, peace and mercy be upon them, and upon the Israel of God" (Gal. 6:15, 16).

In Ephesians 4:4–6 the sevenfold "unity of the Spirit" that makes Jew and Gentile one is given by Paul. Write down each of the seven aspects:

This is the basis of the unity of the church, which is an expression of the unity of God Himself. Such unity is that for which Christ prayed in John 17:20–23. It is the unity that causes the world to believe the witness of the church to Jesus Christ, that He indeed was sent by the Father as the Savior of all people.

The marvelous mercy and infinite wisdom of God is dramatically evident in His dealing with His people. His inclusive kingdom does not obliterate divinely created differences. It transcends them! In Christ, as in marriage, "two become one" without either losing their distinctiveness. Jew and Gentile, male and female, together are needed to reflect the creative and redemptive mercy and wisdom of God. In divinely initiated and sustained unity, God's marvelous mercy and infinite wisdom are seen in vivid contrast to all human efforts to enforce artificial uniformity. God's kingdom transcends human categories of Jewishness and Gentileness. When His kingdom comes, it transforms human categories into divine colors reflecting the wideness of the rainbow of His mercy. When His will is done on earth as it is in heaven, heaven comes to earth and in the church is revealed the manifold wisdom of God.

 FAITH ALIVE

The yearning for unity is expressed in the motto "E Pluribus Unum" (out of many, one) of the United States. It is found in similar mottoes in other countries, as well as in the names of countries such as the "United Kingdom," the "United Arab Emirates" and the former "Union of Soviet Socialist Republics." That this yearning is universal is reflected, of course, in the name given to the international organization of nations pledged to promote peace and security around the world—the "United Nations." Our own families, like the family of nations, yearn for such unity as well. This yearning comes from God Himself who created us in His image to reflect His unity here on earth. If God created this universal yearning, whether national or personal, can He not fulfill it? Indeed He can! Indeed He is . . . in *His* family! The church is a "preview of coming attractions" when all things shall be united in Christ (Eph. 1:9, 10). All sin has disrupted; grace shall unite. And this process of making "out of many, one" begins with becoming "one" with the Lord through forgiveness of sin based on Christ's "at-one-ment" on the Cross. It continues through becoming "one" in heart and mind with brothers and sisters in Christ, especially those within our immediate family: husbands and wives, parents and children.

Lesson 13/Kingdom Hope and Timing

Why does it take God so long to accomplish His redemptive purposes? Why does He seem so slow to bring about His deliverance? Is it God's problem or ours? Is He slow to hear and answer? Does He lack persistence? Or is it we who are slow to listen and respond? Is it we who become weary in waiting and give up?

Ours is not the first generation to wonder about such questions. Israel wondered if they would ever see God's rule and Ruler come. In Peter's day some not only wondered, but they scoffingly asked: "Where is the promise of His [second] coming? For since the fathers fell asleep, all things continue as *they were* from the beginning of creation" (2 Pet. 3:4). Ah, but all things have *not* continued as they were from the beginning, argues the apostle Peter. Look at what God did through the Flood in Noah's day!

Could it be we tend to forget that God has, indeed, been at work in past history? Could it be we have missed seeing God at work as He faithfully laid the necessary foundations and constructed the essential backgrounds for "the fullness of times"? To avoid this error, we have taken the previous lessons to study these necessary foundations and essential backgrounds of God's kingdom. His creative sovereignty, redemptive love and seeming silence have prepared the way for us to understand and appreciate the significance and necessity of His kingdom rule among people.

Now let's read 2 Peter 3:9, 10 and jot down the two points the apostle Peter makes as to how we are to understand God's apparent "slowness" in fulfilling His promise:

2 Pet. 3:9

2 Pet. 3:10

DEFINING THE HOPE
(Matthew 3:2; 4:17)

The focus of this lesson will be a study of the terminology of the kingdom found in the New Testament. How was *kingdom* used and understood by John the Baptist? by Jesus? by the apostle John? by the apostle Paul? Were there other terms used to define and describe the "kingdom"? What are they, and how are they to be understood?

"Repent, for the kingdom of heaven is at hand!" This was the message of both John the Baptist and Jesus Himself (Matt. 3:2; 4:17). With this dramatic announcement by John and Jesus, the use of the words *kingdom, kingdom of heaven,* and *kingdom of God* become frequent in the Gospels, especially in the first three Gospels called the "synoptic" Gospels (Greek: "seeing together," "a similar perspective"). Such occurrences of the word *kingdom* are found 54 times in Matthew, 19 times in Mark, and 44 times in Luke, for a total of 117 times. In John, "kingdom" appears five times. And of these occurrences in the Gospels, about one hundred are found on the lips of Jesus Himself. However, such usage of the word *kingdom* is much less frequent in the rest of the New Testament, occurring a total of only thirty-three times.

The great challenge is to understand what Jesus meant by the word *kingdom,* for nowhere did He define it clearly. Further, what Jesus meant by the word and what was popularly understood by Jesus' contemporaries were not necessarily the same. So let's look up the following passages and write down the contrast between the popular understanding and Jesus' understanding of the *kingdom:*

POPULAR JESUS'
UNDERSTANDING UNDERSTANDING

Luke 17:20, 21

John 6:10–15, 26

John 18:10, 11, 36

Acts 1:6, 7

Where do you think the Jews got such an earthly and nationalistic understanding of the kingdom? Was it totally wrong? What was right? Why?

And where do you think Jesus got His understanding of the kingdom? (Luke 10:8–11, 18–24).

It is clear that Jesus' understanding of the kingdom He announced was not the same as the popular conception. His kingdom had more to do with authority than territory. It had more to do with power than real estate. It had more to do with spiritual than political liberation. Look up John 8:31–36. How did Jesus define true freedom?

Perhaps the most important key in understanding Jesus' view of the kingdom is to understand His view of redemptive history. Like all good Jews, Jesus understood there were two ages: this present age and the age to come (Matt. 12:32; Luke 18:29, 30; John 12:25). But Jesus had a view of the kingdom that seemed to integrate both the prophetic view and the apocalyptic view found in the Old Testament in such passages as Isaiah 9:6, 7 and Daniel 7:13, 14. The kingdom of God would involve both earthly and heavenly dimensions (see Lesson 3). As a result, Jesus seemed to indicate the kingdom was both here and not here. It was both now and not yet. It was both present and yet promised. Take a look at each of these passages and write down that which is both available now and yet is still in the future, noting especially the contrast between the present and future tenses of the verbs:

	PRESENT (NOW)	FUTURE (NOT YET)
COMPARE		
Matt. 8:11 and 21:31, 32		
Matt. 5:6, 10 and 7:21		
Matt. 5:19, 20 and 6:33		
Luke 19:9 and Matt. 10:22		
John 5:25 and 5:28, 29		
John 3:14–16 and Luke 5:29, 30		

Jesus taught that the kingdom and its blessings are available now, and yet they are still promised in the future. What was promised in the future is now available in the present. A "now, not yet" tension seems to exist in Jesus' teaching about the kingdom. The kingdom is today, yet it is also tomorrow. The kingdom is present, yet promised. "Fulfillment of the OT hope without apocalyptic consummation" seems to be Jesus' view of redemptive history. It represents a radical modification of the views of His contemporaries. Jesus taught that the future righteous age of God's rule has come into this age in an unexpected manner. The kingdom of God is now, yet it is future. Such a perspective is called "eschatological dualism." The future eschatological age (Greek, *eschaton*, "last things") has invaded this present age, making available the blessings of the future age now . . . at least in part. Thus an "overlap of the ages" has occurred. Two ages are occurring simultaneously. And this has happened because something significant has taken place. The King has come! Thus, the kingdom has come.

 BEHIND THE SCENES

The discussion about the kingdom of God as present or future, earthly or heavenly, political or spiritual, ideal or real, now or not yet, continues. Literature on the subject abounds. Several books focus the issues in a most helpful manner. For further study several books are recommended. They are considered to be "classics" on the subject, focusing the issues in a most helpful manner:

John Bright, *The Kingdom of God* (Abingdon Press, 1953)

E. Stanley Jones, *The Unshakeable Kingdom and the Unchangeable Person* (Abingdon Press, 1972)

George E. Ladd, *The Gospel of the Kingdom* (Eerdmans, 1959)

"KINGDOM OF HEAVEN" OR "KINGDOM OF GOD" (Matthew 19:23, 24)

 KINGDOM EXTRA

Synonymous Expressions. Matthew 19:23, 24 uses the phrases "kingdom of heaven" and "kingdom of God" interchangeably. In doing so, it sufficiently demonstrates that the two terms are meant to refer to one and the same thing: the kingdom. Although some make a labored distinction between them, this text and ten others in the Gospels clearly show that the "kingdom of heaven" and "kingdom of God" are verifiably synonyms. Matthew is the only New Testament writer who used the term "kingdom of heaven." Doing so, he showed a sensitivity toward his originally intended audience of Jewish readers, for whom too frequent a use of the name of "God" would have seemed irreverent. By a variety of terms Matthew refers to "the kingdom" fifty times in his Gospel: thirty-two times as "kingdom of heaven"; five times as "kingdom of God"; four times as the "Father's" kingdom; and twice as the kingdom of "the Son of Man." The remaining seven references are simply to "the kingdom" without other designation. This variety in the usage, made by the only one using the phrase "kingdom of heaven," surely shows these terms to be synonyms for the kingdom.

"THE KINGDOM NOW/NOT YET"
(Luke 17:20–30)

Jesus said the kingdom is at hand, indicating its accessibility. He also stated that the "time was fulfilled," indicating the time is now—present-tense now.

WORD WEALTH

Time, *kairos.* Indicates a fixed season, an opportune time, an appointed period, a definitive time. It describes a kind or quality of time calling for appropriate action. *Chronos* signifies a period, duration, or quantity of time. It is the word from which we derive the English word *chronology.*

Clearly the note of fulfillment is evident in Jesus' proclamation. The word used for "time" is *kairos,* which points toward a set season and calls for a proper response, because the time of fulfillment ("filling full") has arrived. The kingdom of God has drawn near. Therefore, the call is for repentance and faith. We discussed briefly this call to repentance and its "fruit" in Lesson 11. The call that follows— to "believe the gospel"—is the new element in Jesus' proclamation. John the Baptist had pointed to Jesus as "greater" although he came before Him. Jesus was the One whose coming occasioned this time of "fulfillment," because He was the One who brought the kingdom as the messianic king of David's line. Thus, the coming of the Messiah, Jesus Christ, brought a special "*kairos* moment" that demanded an appropriate response.

BEHIND THE SCENES

Paul writes in Galatians 4:4 that "when the fullness of the time [*chronos*] had come, God sent forth His Son, born of a woman . . . " In what sense was 6–5 B.C. the right time for Jesus to be born? Only God really knows the meaning of "the fullness of the time." But from the earth side of things there are a number of reasons that suggest that Christ's birth at this point in human history was most strategic in terms of the preparation occasioned by the Jewish religion, the Greek culture, and the Roman government.

First, the Jews were highly expectant as they anticipated the renewal of the prophetic word after four hundred years of silence. Further, God's people were well prepared to pay attention to a message of grace and forgiveness, for the legalism of the Pharisees had become so burdensome few even attempted to keep all the Law. Also, the Jewish Diaspora (dispersion) had scattered Jews throughout the Roman Empire with nearly 80% living outside of Israel. Thus, the development of the synagogue with its emphasis on the teaching of the Law of Moses was necessary to perpetuate the Jewish faith since it was too far for most Jews to travel to Jerusalem for worship and sacrifice at the temple.

Second, the Greek, or Hellenistic, culture broke down the barriers between Greeks and Jews who lived in the Diaspora where all spoke the same Greek language and many Jews adopted a Hellenistic life-style. Further, Hellenistic culture gave the world one known language and thus greatly aided communication throughout the Roman Empire. Also, the translation of the Hebrew Scriptures into Greek (the *Septuagint,* or *LXX*) during the third century B.C. made it possible for many Greeks to understand the Jewish faith and its hope of a Messiah.

Third, the rule of the Romans brought about a time of enforced "peace" called *Pax Romana* (Roman Peace) which allowed the free flow of ideas. Further, the Romans built an amazing network of "Roman Roads" which linked the empire. Also, the Romans allowed the practice of "legal religions" of which Judaism was one. Since the Romans viewed Christianity as a "sect of Judaism" they permitted this new faith to be practiced legally and did not consistently oppose or persecute Christians until near the end of the first century A.D. By then the church was strong enough to survive and to spread, even when persecuted. Thus, the way was strategically prepared for the birth of Christ and the spread of the good news of the gospel at this "hinge point" of "the fullness of time" nearly 2,000 years ago.

"The kingdom of God is at hand," declared Jesus. But how near is "at hand"? We have just looked at how Jesus transformed the Old Testament hope. He taught that the kingdom had come in fulfillment of the Old Testament hope, but without full consummation, which was yet future. Although God's salvation through His anointed Messiah was one act—His act—it would be played out in two scenes upon the stage of human history. And so the Messiah came the first time almost incognito as a suffering Servant in anticipation of His second coming in triumphant glory as "King of kings and Lord of lords." The Lion of the tribe of Judah came first as the Lamb of God to take away the sin of the world. Thus, "at hand" really consisted of "two hands." God's kingdom would "come near" at two moments in history.

Let's take a look at Luke 17:20–30 and look at these "two moments." When asked by the Pharisees "when the kingdom of God would come," how did Jesus answer? (vv. 20, 21)

What does this mean? The nature of the kingdom is such that it can sneak up on you. It does not come "with observation." In fact, it is "within" or "in the midst of" you. Whether the meaning of the word is "in you" or "among you," the point is clear. God's kingdom is not an outward, visible, observable kingdom as had been anticipated by the Jews. Thus, it could be "at hand" or "near" and be missed.

Jesus then explained to His disciples about another future coming of the kingdom "when the Son of Man is revealed" (v. 30). "But first He must suffer many things and be rejected by this generation" (v. 25). Then there would come a "day" of the Son of Man that would be as observable as the Flood in Noah's day and the destruction of Sodom and Gomorrah in Lot's day. And although false prophets would lead some people astray, apparently for the watchful and discerning person there would be "signs" that would enable them to prepare properly for this "[day] of the Son of Man" (vv. 23, 24). In fact, Jesus said that, as it was in the days of Noah and Lot, so would it be in the days of the Son of Man. Look at verses 26–30 and list the common characteristics of their days with the day when the Son of Man is revealed:

"As it was in the days of Noah":

"As it was in the days of Lot":

What seems to be the focus of the things described by Jesus? Is it on the dramatic increase of wickedness or the undramatic continuation of normal life-activities? If it is the latter, which it probably is, then the Second Coming of the Messiah could sneak up on people as did the Flood and Sodom's destruction. How can such observable and dramatic events catch people off guard? It is because they missed "hearing the voice of God" calling them to prepare before these great events occurred. It is because they missed "first comings" that they were unprepared for the "second coming." The Scripture is clear: God "does nothing, unless He reveals His secret to His servants the prophets" (Amos 3:7) who then issue a call to people to "prepare to meet [their] God" (Amos 4:12). God mercifully gives opportunity for people to prepare for divine appointments.

The "observable" and visible kingdom or rule of God was anticipated in the first coming of the rule of God in Jesus

Christ. In mercy God wants people prepared for His all-encompassing sovereign rule and thus He has sent His Son to prepare the way. He even sent John the Baptist to prepare the way of the One who prepares the way!—so great is His mercy and kindness! The kingdom is "now . . . not yet" for a very practical purpose—proper preparation! And this preparation means actual participation, at least in part, of all the blessings which will characterize God's kingdom at its future consummation. The "first course" of the "menu" of the great marriage supper of the Lamb is now available! Forgiveness, peace, joy, healing, freedom, and love are ours now in anticipation of the coming glory of God's kingdom rule.

When will God's kingdom rule come about? Jesus used the analogy of a woman in labor in Matthew 24:8 where the word "sorrows" is literally the word for "labor pains." Anticipating His coming notes events, which, like labor pains, can tell us the "birth" (His coming) is imminent, but they cannot tell us the time of the birth. An increase in both the intensity and rapidity of the labor pains will signal the end of this age and the birth of the age to come just as increased labor pains indicate the end of pregnancy and the birth of a child. Therefore, we had best be "about the Father's business" as we await the end of the age for He *alone* knows when the "baby" will be born! For further study on this matter of the time of prophetic consummation, you may wish to consult such books as *Dreams, Visions and Oracles: the Laymen's Guide to Biblical Prophecy*, edited by Carl E. Armerding and W. Ward Gasque (Baker, 1977); *The Blessed Hope*, by George E. Ladd (Eerdmans, 1956); and *Armageddon Now!* by Dwight Wilson (Baker, 1977).

UNIVERSAL PROCLAMATION OF THE KINGDOM
(Matthew 24:14; 25:31–46)

"This gospel of the kingdom will be preached in all the world as a witness to all the nations, and then the end will come," declared Jesus. Please describe the essential elements which make up this final sign (Matt. 24:14).

The message is "this gospel of the kingdom." Can you define it in a sentence or two?

It will be preached "in all the world [the inhabited earth] . . . to all the nations," (*ethne* means "ethnic/cultural groups)." Why both "in" and "to"?

It will be "preached . . . as a witness." Why "as a witness"? What does "witness" mean?

This is the only sign that appears to have a "conditional element" of human responsibility within it. In other words, the end will come when Christ's last commission to make disciples of all nations is completed, and that depends on the disciples' obedient participation in being His "witnesses to . . . the end of the earth" after the Holy Spirit has come upon them" (Acts 1:8).

The evangelization of all nations is assumed by Jesus in His teaching about the end. Note the universal motif found throughout His discourse. Write down what it says about "all nations" in each of these verses:

Matt. 24:9

Matt. 24:30

Matt. 25:32

Let's take a careful look at the parable of the judgment of the nations in Matthew 25:31–46, which concludes Jesus' "Olivet Discourse."

 FAITH ALIVE

Maranatha is not a Greek word. It is a transliteration of an Aramaic word meaning "Our Lord, come." It is found in 1 Corinthians 16:22 and reflects the cry of the church for the return of Christ. Also found at the end of the Book of Revelation, it is the yearning of the bride for the Bridegroom: "Even so, come, Lord Jesus!" (Rev. 22:20). From the earliest days of the church, there has been an eager longing for the speedy return of the Lord. And so we today who are also members of the bride of Christ likewise yearn and long to see the Bridegroom face to face! We, too, cry, "Maranatha!"

But there is another yearning. It is the yearning of God Himself. We have seen how the Father has patiently sought to win back a wayward race since the time of the Fall in Eden. So great was His love that in the fullness of time He sent His only Son, Jesus Christ. The Father is not willing any should perish. He wants all to come to repentance. Thus He made full provision for the salvation of all in the death and resurrection of His Son. Therefore, He yearns for all to have opportunity to hear of His great gift so His family can be completed . . . finally.

O Father, with our yearning for Your kingdom to come and Your will to be done fully and finally, may we share Your yearning to see people of every tongue, tribe, kindred, and nation come into Your kingdom and do Your will. Fulfill Your yearning through us that You might fulfill the yearning in us for Your Son's soon return. For Yours is the kingdom and the power and the glory forever and ever! Amen and amen.